The International JOKE Dictionary

* * * * *

How to raise a laugh in five languages

WOLFE PUBLISHING LTD
10 Earlham Street, London WC2

Uniform with this volume
THE INSULT DICTIONARY
THE LOVER'S DICTIONARY

SBN 72340124 1

Printed in Great Britain by The Whitefriars Press Ltd,
London & Tonbridge

CONTENTS

INTRODUCTION

VISUAL HUMOUR cuts through international boundaries like a hot knife through butter. The comedies of Mack Sennett, Charlie Chaplin, Laurel and Hardy and the Three Stooges can be shown on any cinema or T.V. screen in the world and get a laugh.

But verbal humour smacks straight away into the language barrier. Not even Bob Hope would raise a titter if he stood up and wisecracked in English in Novosibirsk. Nor would he do much better if he delivered his jokes in a straight Russian translation: things which are funny in America may not be at all funny in Russia, and vice versa.

An American comedian, for instance, can make jokes about deep freezes, drive-in cinemas, and central heating. An audience in a country where none of these things existed would be left wondering what the man was going on about. Commercial traveller jokes may be hilariously funny in countries where he is a familiar figure. In countries which have never seen a commercial traveller, the joke suddenly has no point.

For a joke to translate, therefore, it must be:

(a) Basic, and

(b) Given a free, and not literal, translation.

This we have tried to do, choosing those jokes which apply to the universal human condition—man and wife jokes, drinking jokes, etc.—and which do not rely for their appeal on a special set of local circumstances.

True, there are jokes which mention trains, cars and planes. But very few people in the world have not at least seen these.

We have chosen translators, too, for their sense of humour and their knowledge of the up-to-date idiom of their native language, rather than for their pure academic ability (they have this, of course, in full measure, but it would be useless without the other attributes).

So now we have a book which, we hope, will enable you to raise a giggle in any part of the world where the five languages are spoken.

Remember, in the telling, to adapt your delivery to the national characteristics of the listener.

In telling a joke to a **German**, for instance, the delivery should be loud, robust, and not too fast. It is permissible, in German, to laugh heartily at one's own joke. (This is also a help to the listener—at least he knows then when you've reached the punch line.)

In **French**, the delivery should be saucy, with lots of eye rolling, eyebrow waggling and a few Chevalier-type throaty chortles.

Italian jokes are accompanied by plenty of flamboyant gestures, lots of *simpatico* and as much expression as you can muster.

Spanish jokes come over best with a dignified, but explosive delivery. Although you are the funny man, the dignity must still be there. You must lead on the listener as the matador leads on the bull—and hope for a laugh at the moment of truth. (You should get one: the Spaniards are much too polite to let you die the death.)

If you do die the death, in any of the languages, you can blame it on the jokes. We'd hate you to think that you were a lousy comedian.

NOTES ON PRONUNCIATION
by the translators

FRENCH. The English stiff upper lip is just too stiff to bend itself to French vowels, except after years of practice and Pernod—and even then it will betray itself, but here are a few notes that may help.

Where there is 'u' in French, or 'ure' this should come out as 'i' in 'bit' (*not* in bite).

The French 'j' must be pronounced fairly lightly as the second 'g' in 'garage'.

The 'e', 'eu' and 'eur' sounds go in as 'er' or 'ehr'—quite easy, if you lengthen them a bit. 'Euse' becomes like 'ehrz'.

The 'ail' sound is the hardest to imitate, the nearest to it is 'aaee' or 'aee'—but the ee must not be stressed.

'En', 'em', 'in', 'im', 'ein' and 'un' all go in as 'an' or 'am'. You can get away with it in the heat of the moment.

'Oi' is like 'w' but everybody knows 'oui oui'. Finally, all would-be French speakers are reminded that in this delightful language *all* words are stressed on the last syllable, whatever the length, and that a nasal sound and high speed can cover a multitude of linguistic sins.

GERMAN. The German double-letter 'β' is replaced here by 'ss'. Other usages are:

ch: pronounce as ch in 'loch'
g: prounounce hard, as in 'gay'
i: short, as in 'fit'
y: pronounce as in 'fly'
ao: as in 'owl'

ITALIAN. Most consonants are pronounced as in English. The following are the main exceptions:

c and *cc* before *e* and *i* = CH as in CHurch
before *a, o* and *u* = C as in Cake.
ch = K as in Key.
ci before *a, o* and *u* = CH as in CHocolate.
g and *gg* before *e* or *i* = G as in General.
g before *a, o* or *u* = G as in Goat.
gh before *e* and *i* = G as in Get.
gl before *i* = LL as in miLLion.
gn = N as in oNion.
sc before *e* or *i* = SH as in SHave.
sch = SK as in SKittle.
sci before *a, o, u* = SH as in SHape.
zz = TS as in caTS.

Vowel Sounds

a = A as in fAther.
e = E open as in pEt; closed as in gAte.
i = I as in machIne.
o = O open as in pOt; closed as in pOst.
u = OO as in cOOl.

SPANISH. *á* or *ah* is pronounced as the English *a* in *car*. (Never like *all, dare, gave*.)

é or *eh* is always like the English *e* in *set, let, wet*. (Never like *me, here, become*.)

ó or *oh* has the sound of English *o* in *lord* or English *aw* in *law*. (Never like *old, go, ago*.)

i has the sound of *i* in *bit*. (Never of *I*, mine, island.)

y has the sound of *y* in *yes, yawn*, or the *e* in *me*. (Never like *my, by, cry*.)

th has the sound of English *th* in *thing*. (Never of *the, that, this*.)

EATING YOUR WORDS

	GERMAN
'Waiter! There's a fly in my soup!' 'Don't make a fuss—they'll all want one.'	'Ober! In meiner Suppe ist eine Fliege!' 'Nicht so laut, sonst will jeder eine haben.'
'Waiter! There's a fly in my soup!' 'Don't worry, sir, there's a spider on the bread.'	'Ober! In meiner Suppe ist eine Fliege!' 'Keine Aufregung, mein Herr, da sitzt eine Spinne auf dem Brot.'
'Waiter! There's a dead fly in my soup!' 'Yes, sir, it's the heat that kills them.'	'Ober! In meiner Suppe ist eine tote Fliege.' 'Kein Wunder, mein Herr, die Suppe ist sehr heiss.'
'Waiter! This coffee tastes like cocoa!' 'I'm sorry, sir. I must have given you tea.'	'Ober! Dieser Kaffee schmeckt wie Kakao!' 'Verzeihen Sie, mein Herr, ich glaube, ich habe Ihnen Tee gegeben.'
'Waiter! How did this fly get into my soup?' 'I think it flew in, sir.'	'Ober! Wie kommt diese Fliege in meine Suppe?' 'Sie ist sicherlich hineingeflogen, mein Herr.'
'Waiter! Have you got frogs' legs?' 'No, sir. I always walk like this.'	'Herr Ober, haben Sie Froschschenkel?' 'Nein, mein Herr, ich gehe so.'

FRENCH	ITALIAN	SPANISH
'Garçon! Il y a une mouche dans ma soupe!' 'N'en faites pas une histoire, Monsieur, ou ils vont tous en vouloir une!'	'Cameriere! C'è una mosca nella minestra!' 'Non faccia storie, se no ne vogliono una tutti.'	—¡Camarero! ¡Hay una mosca en la sopa! —¡No lo diga tan alto! Todos van a querer una.
'Garçon! Il y a une mouche dans ma soupe!' 'Ne vous affolez pas, Monsieur, il y une araignée sur le pain!'	'Cameriere! C'è una mosca nella minestra!' 'Signore, non si preoccupi, c'è un ragno sul pane!'	—¡Camarero! ¡Hay una mosca en la sopa! —¡No se preocupe, señor! En el pan hay una araña.
'Garçon! Il y a une mouche qui est morte dans ma soupe!' 'Malheureusement, Monsieur, c'est la chaleur qui les tue!'	'Cameriere! C'è una mosca morta nella mia minestra!' 'Si, signore, è il caldo che le uccide!'	—¡Camarero! ¡Hay una mosca muerta en la sopa! —Sí, señor. Es el calor que las mata.
'Garçon! Ce café a ungoût de cacao!' 'Mille excuses, Monsieur. J'ai dû vous servir du thé!'	'Cameriere! Questo caffè ha gusto di cacao!' 'Oh, signore, mi dispiace. Devo averle dato il tè!'	—¡Camarero! ¡Este café sabe a cacao! —Lo siento, señor. Debo haberle servido té.
'Garçon! Expliquez-moi comment cette mouche est arrivée dans ma soupe?' 'Elle a dû y atterrir, Monsieur!'	'Cameriere! Com'è finita nella mia minestra questa mosca?' 'Credo che vi sia arrivata a volo, signore!'	—¡Camarero! ¿Cómo llegó esta mosca a mi sopa? —Creo que volando, señor.
'Garçon! Vous avez des cuisses de grenouille?' 'Non, Monsieur. Je marche toujours comme ça.'	'Cameriere! Ha delle gambe di rana?' 'No, signore. Cammino sempre cosí.'	—¡Camarero! ¿Tiene usted ancas de rana? —No, señor. Siempre ando de esta manera.

	GERMAN
'Waiter! This soup isn't fit for a pig!' 'I'm sorry, sir. I'll take it away and get some that is.'	'Ober! Diese Suppe können Sie doch keinem Schwein anbieten!' 'Moment, ich bringe eine andere, von der können Sie das nicht sagen.'
'Waiter! You've got your thumb in my soup!' 'Don't worry, sir, it's not very hot.'	'Ober, Ihr Daumen ist in meiner Suppe!' 'Keine Sorge, mein Herr, sie ist nicht heiss.'
'Waiter! Do you serve crabs?' 'Take a seat, sir. We serve anybody.'	'Herr Ober, servieren Sie auch Hammel?' 'Aber gewiss, mein Herr, nehmen Sie Platz, hier wird jeder bedient.'
Then there was the man who went on a five-day fast. He didn't intend to—he just couldn't catch the waiter's eye.	Dann war da noch der Mann, der fünf Tage lang fastete. Unfreiwillig, weil der Kellner über ihn hinwegsah.
'Waiter,' said the annoyed diner. 'Why has this lobster only one claw?' 'It lost the other one in a fight, sir,' said the waiter superciliously. 'So it lost it in a fight—so take it away and bring me the winner!'	'Ober, warum hat dieser Hummer nur eine Zange?' fragte der Gast ungeduldig. 'Die andere hat er im Kampf verloren,' sagte der Kellner oberflächlich. 'So, so. Dann bringen Sie mir gefälligst den Sieger.'

FRENCH	ITALIAN	SPANISH
'Garçon! C'est même pas une soupe pour un cochon!' 'Mille excuses, Monsieur. Je vais vous apporter une qui le soit.'	'Cameriere! Questa minestra non è degna di un maiale!' 'Mi dispiace signore. Gliela porto via e gliene porto un'altra che lo sia.'	—¡Camarero! !Esta sopa no vale (ni) para un cerdo! —Lo siento, señor. Le traeré algo más adecuado.
'Garçon! Vous avez trempé votre pouce dans ma soupe!' 'Ne vous inquiétez pas, Monsieur, elle n'est pas brûlante.'	'Cameriere! Ha il pollice nella mia minestra!' 'Non si preoccupi, signore, non è molto calda.'	—¡Camarero! ¡Ha metido el dedo en la sopa! —Descuide, señor. No está muy caliente.
'Garçon! Vous servez des crabes?' 'Asseyez-vous, Monsieur. Ici, nous servons n'importe qui!'	'Cameriere, servite gamberi?' 'Si accomodi, signore. Serviamo chiunque.'	—¡Camarero! ¿Sirve usted cangrejos? —Tome asiento, señor. Servimos a todo el mundo.
Un homme a jeûné une fois pendant cinq jours. Ce n'est pas qu'il voulait le faire; simplement, il n'est pas arrivé à attirer l'attention du garçon.	Poi c'era quel tale che si mise a fare un digiuno di cinque giorni. Non che ne avesse la minima intenzione —semplicemente non riusciva a farsi notare dal cameriere.	Hubo un hombre que ayunó cinco días. No lo hizo adrede. Es que no logró atraer la atención del camarero.
'Garçon!' dit le client mécontent. 'Pourquoi ce homard n'a qu'une pince?' 'Il a perdu l'autre dans une bagarre, Monsieur,' répondit le garçon d'un ton dédaigneux. 'Ah bon? Alors enlevez-moi ça d'ici et apportez-moi le vainqueur!'	'Cameriere,' esclamò il cliente arrabbiato, 'perché quest'aragosta ha una pinza sola?' 'Perché l'altra, signore, l'ha persa in combattimento,' rispose altezzosamente il cameriere. 'L'ha persa in combattimento? Allora portala via, voglio il vincitore.'	—Camarero —exclamó el cliente desolado—. ¿Por qué tiene esta langosta una sola pata? —Perdió la otra peleando, señor —respondió el camarero reticente. —¿Con que la perdió peleando, eh? ¡Pues tráigame a la vencedora!

EATING YOUR WORDS

GERMAN

Impatient diner: 'Are you the same waiter I gave my order to?'
Slow waiter: 'Yes, sir.'
Impatient diner: 'Funny. I was expecting a much older man.'

Der ungeduldige Gast: 'Sind Sie der Ober, dem ich meine Bestellung gegeben habe?'
Der langsame Kellner: 'Ja, mein Herr.'
Der ungeduldige Gast: 'Komisch. Sie müssten doch viel älter sein.'

ONE OVER THE EIGHT

Every day the man walked into the bar, asked for a glass of water, drank it and walked out. It went on for so long that the barman was getting annoyed.
'Look here,' he said after the third week, 'every day you come in here, ask for a glass of water, drink it and walk out.'
'What do you expect me to do,' said the man: 'Stagger?'

Jeden Tag kommt der Mann in die Bar, bestellt ein Glas Wasser, trink es und geht wieder hinaus. Das wurde dem Barkeeper schliesslich nach drei Wochen zu dumm:
'Hören Sie 'mal, Sie können doch nicht hier jeden Tag erscheinen, ein Glas Wasser trinken und wieder hinausgehen.'
'Was erwarten Sie sonst? Soll ich hinaustorkeln?'

The drunk was stopped by a policeman as he staggered about the High Street at three o'clock in the morning.
'Can you explain why you're out at this time?' asked the policeman.
'If I could,' said the drunk, 'I'd be home by now.'

Ein Betrunkener schwankt morgens um drei Uhr die Hauptstrasse entlang und wird von einem Polizisten angehalten.
'Können Sie mir erklären, was Sie hier um diese Zeit machen?'
'Wenn ich das könnte,' sagte der Betrunkene, 'dann wäre ich längst zuhaus.'

FRENCH	ITALIAN	SPANISH
Le client impatient: 'Etes-vous le même garçon à qui j'ai dicté ma commande?' Le garçon indolent: 'Oui, Monsieur.' Le client impatient: 'Curieux. Je m'attendais à ce que vous ayiez veilli entretemps.'	Il cliente impaziente: 'Lei è lo stesso cameriere che ha preso il mio ordine?' Il cameriere lento: 'Sissignore.' Il cliente impaziente: Strano! Mi aspettavo un uomo molto piû anziano.'	Cliente apresurado: —¿Es usted el camarero al que hice mi encargo? Camarero indolente: —Sí, señor. Cliente apresurado: —¡Qué extraño! Esperaba encontrarle mucho más viejo!
Chaque jour, l'homme entrait dans le bar, demandait un verre d'eau, le buvait et s'en allait. Ce manège dura si longtemps que le barman finit par se mettre en colère. 'Dites-donc!' fit-il après avoir patienté trois semaines, 'chaque jour vous entrez ici, vous demandez un verre d'eau, vous le buvez et puis vous repartez comme si de rien n'était.' 'Qu'est-ce que vous voulez que je fasse?' répondit l'homme, 'Que je sorte en titubant?'	Ogni giorno un tizio entrava in un bar, chiedeva un bicchier d'acqua, lo beveva e se ne andava. Alla fine, il cameriere si stufò. 'Senta un po',' disse dopo la terza settimana, 'ogni giorno lei entra, chiede un bicchier d'acqua, lo beve e esce.' 'E che vorrebbe che facessi?' rispose l'uomo,' che cadessi in terra ubriaco?'	Un hombre entraba cada día en el bar, pedía un vaso de agua, se lo bebía y salía otra vez. Lo hizo tantas veces que el barman empezaba a cansarse. —Veamos dijo al cabo de la tercera semana—. Cada día viene usted aquí, se bebe un vaso de agua y se va tan tranquilo . . . —¿Y qué esperaba usted? —repuso el hombre—. ¿Que me tambalease?
Trois heures du matin. L'agent de police arrêta le soûlard qui navigait d'un trottoir à l'autre, dans la Grand 'Rue. 'Pouvez-vous me dire ce que vous faites fans la rue à une heure aussi tardive?' demanda l'agent de police. 'Si j'pouvais vous expliquer ça,' répondit le soûlard, 'je serais déjà chez moi à cette heure-ci.'	Un ubriaco barcollante fu fermato da un poliziotto per la strada alle tre di mattina. 'Mi sa dire che cosa fa fuori a quest'ora?' chiese il poliziotto. 'Se lo sapessi,' disse l'ubriaco, 'a quest'ora sarei già a casa.'	El borracho fué detenido por un guardia cuando daba traspiés por High Street a las tres de la madrugada. —¿Puede decirme por qué anda a estas horas por la calle? —le preguntó el policía. —Si pudiera hacerlo —contestó el borracho—, no estaría aquí, sino en mi casa.

GERMAN

The drunk got home in the small hours of the morning, fumbled with his latch-key and finally got inside.
The noise awakened his wife.
'Henry!' she called from the bedroom. 'Is that you?'
'Just a minute,' said Henry, and staggered to the mirror in the hallway. He took a long, hard look, focusing through bleary eyes. After a few minutes he was satisfied.
'Yes,' he called back. 'It's me all right.'

Ein Betrunkener kommt mitten in der Nacht nach Haus und fummelt eine ganze Weile mit dem Schlüssel an der Wohnungstür herum. Schliesslich hat er sie geöffnet.
'Harry, bist Du's?' ruft seine Frau, die von dem Lärm aufgewacht ist.
'Moment mal,' ruft Harry zurück und torkelt zum Spiegel in der Halle, fixiert sich mit verschwommenen Augen eine Weile und ruft dann glücklich: 'Ja, ich bin's!'

The centenarian was asked by the newspaper man for the secret of his longevity.
'I have never taken strong liquor, never gambled, never played around with women.'
Suddenly from the next room. there was a great crash and a female scream.
'What on earth's that?' asked the newspaperman.
'It's my father,' said the old man. 'He got back from the races, drunk as a lord, and he's chasing the maid again.'

Der Reporter fragte den Hunderjährigen nach dem Geheimnis seiner Langlebigkeit.
'Ich habe nie getrunken, nie gespielt und keine Frauengeschichten gehabt.'
Plötzlich kam vom Nebenzimmer ein lautes Getöse und der Schrei einer Frau.
'Was ist denn da los?' fragte der Reporter.
'Mein Vater. Der ist wieder völlig betrunken vom Rennplatz zurückgekommen und jetzt ist er wieder hinter dem Hausmädchen her.'

FRENCH	ITALIAN	SPANISH
Le soûlard arriva chez lui aux premières heures du matin, tâtonna avec sa clé pour trouver le trou de la serrure et réussit finalement à rentrer chez lui. Le bruit qu'il fit réveilla son épouse. 'Henry,' cria-t-elle de la chambre à coucher, 'c'est toi?' 'Un instant,' répondit Henry, et il se dirigea en titubant vers le miroir situé dans le hall. D'un oeil aviné, il se regarda longuement, sans complaisance. Après un examen de quelques minutes, il fut satisfait du résultat. 'Oui,' lança-t-il finalement à sa femme, 'c'est moi, c'est bien moi!'	Un ubriaco tornò a casa nelle ore piccole e non senza difficolta infilò la chiave nella toppa e aprí la porta. Il rumore svegliò la moglie. 'Enrico!' gridò dalla camera da letto. 'Sei tu?' 'Un minuto,' disse Enrico e, barcollando, andò davanti allo specchio in anticamera. Si scrutò a lungo con lo sguardo avvinazzato, e dopo qualche minuto, finalmente soddisfatto, disse: 'Sí, sono io, sono proprio io.'	El borracho llegó a su casa a primeras horas de la madrugada, hurgó con la llave y al fin entró. El ruido despertó a su esposa. —¡Enrique! —llamó desde el dormitorio—. ¿Eres tú? —¡Espera un momento! —respondió Enrique, dirigiéndose hacia un espejo. Se miró en él largo rato, tratando de enfocar la imagen. Al cabo de unos minutos se sintió satisfecho. —Sí —repuso entonces—. Soy yo.
Le centenaire confiait au reporter le secret de sa longévité: 'Je n'ai jamais pris d'alcool fort, jamais joué aux jeux de hasard et jamais tourné autour des femmes.' Soudain, de la pièce voisine, on entendit un bruit sourd suivi d'un hurlement de femme. 'Qu'est-ce que c'est que ça?' demanda le reporter. 'C'est mon père,' répondit le centenaire. 'Le voilà qui rentre des courses, rond comme une barrique et qui se met à courir encore après la bonne!'	Ad un centenario alcuni giornalisti stavano chiedendo il segreto della sua longevità. 'Non ho mai bevuto, non ho mai giuocato, e non sono mai stato a donne.' Tutto ad un tratto, dalla stanza accanto, si udí un tonfo ed un urlo di donna. 'Che cosa diamine succede?' domandò uno dei giornalisti. 'È mio padre,' disse il vecchio, 'che come al solito è tornato dalle corse ubriaco fradicio e sta correndo dietro alla serva.'	Un periodista le preguntó al centenario el secreto de su longevidad. —Jamás he tomado bebidas fuertes, no he apostado en mi vida y nunca he perdido la cabeza con las mujeres. De pronto, en la habitación contigua se oyó un gran revuelo y un grito de mujer. —¿Qué ocurre ahí —preguntó el periodista. —Es mi padre —contestó el viejecito—. Ha llegado de las carreras borracho como una cuba y está persiguiendo otra vez a la doncella . . .

GERMAN

Fred opened his eyes and realised he was in hospital. His head was bandaged, his legs were in plaster, one arm was in a sling and his ribs were strapped up. The last thing he could remember was standing in the bar of the local pub with his friend Harry. He turned his head painfully—and there was Harry, sitting by the bed.

'What happened?' asked Fred.

'After twelve Scotches you said you would bet anyone a pound that you could jump off the roof and fly over the town.'

'My God! Why didn't you stop me?'

'I was getting such wonderful odds.'

Fred wacht im Krankenhaus auf. Kopf verbunden, Arm in der Schlinge, Beine in Gips, Rippen bandagiert. Er konnte sich nur noch daran erinnern, dass er mit seinem Freund Harry an der Bar in der Kneipe an der Ecke stand.

Unter Schmerzen drehte er seinen Kopf zur Seite—und da, am Bett, sass Harry.

'Was ist geschehen?' fragte Fred.

'Du hast nach zwölf Whikys zehn Mark gewettet, dass Du vom Dach aus über die Stadt fliegen kannst.'

'Warum hast Du mich dann zum Donnerwetter nicht zurückgehalten?'

'Und die Wette nicht gewinnen?'

The drunk staggered across to his car, dropped his keys, picked them up again and tried vainly to get one of them in the lock. A policeman walked over to him.

'You're surely not hoping to drive that car in your condition,' he said.

'What do you expect me to do?' said the drunk. 'I'm in no fit state to walk.'

Ein Betrunkener steht schwankend an seinem Wagen und bemüht sich vergeblich, die Wagentür zu öffnen. Die Schlüssel fallen ihm immer wieder aus der Hand. Ein Polizist kommt auf ihn zu: 'Sie wollen doch nicht etwa in diesem Zustand den Wagen fahren?'

'Was denn sonst?' fragte der Betrunkene, 'soll ich in diesem Zustand etwa laufen?'

FRENCH

Fred ouvrit les yeux et se rendit compte qu'il était dans un hôpital, la tête entourée de bandages, les deux jambes dans le plâtre, le bras en écharpe et les côtes tout endolories. Tout ce dont il se souvenait c'était qu'il était debout au bar du bistro du coin en compagnie de son ami Harry. Faisant un effort, il parvint à grand'peine à tourner la tête et là, assis à son chevet, il y avait Harry.
'Qu'est-ce qui m'est arrivé?' demanda Fred.
'Après ton douzième whisky, t'as parié mille balles avec n'importe qui que tu sauterais du toit et volerais au-dessus de la ville.'
'Mon Dien! Et tu n'as rien fait pour m'arrêter?'
'Tu penses! J'étais trop occupé; j'avais des paris à des cotes fantastiques!'

ITALIAN

Aprendo gli occhi, Fred si trovò in ospedale. Aveva la testa e le costole bendate, le gambe ingessate, un braccio al collo. L'ultima cosa che ricordava era di essere andato all'osteria con l'amico Harry. Voltò con difficolta la testa—e Harry era lí, accanto al suo letto.
'Cosa è successo?' domandò Fred.
'Dopo dodici bicchieri di whisky hai scommesso una sterlina che saresti saltato dal tetto ed avresti volato sopra la città.'
'Mio Dio! E perché non mi hai fermato?'
'Ero sicuro di vincere la scommessa.'

SPANISH

Fred abrió los ojos y vio que estaba en el hospital. Tenía vendada la cabeza, una pierna enyesada, un brazo en cabestrillo y las costillas con bandas de esparadrapo. Lo último que recordaba era la taberna, a la que había ido con su amigo Harry.
Volvió la cabeza difícilmente . . . y allí estaba Harry, sentado junto a la cama.
—¿Qué ha sucedido? —preguntó Fred.
—Después de tomarte doce whiskies, dijiste que apostabas una libra con cualquiera a que eras capaz de saltar desde el tejado y volar por todo el pueblo.
—¡Santo Dios! ¿Y por qué no me detuviste?
—¡Eran tan estupendas las contraapuestas!

Le soûlard tituba en direction de sa voiture, fit tomber ses clés, les retrouva et tâtonna vainement pour trouver la serrure. Un agent, qui avait suivi la scène, l'aborda.
'Vous n'avez sûrement pas l'intention de conduire votre voiture dans l'état où vous êtes?' dit-il.
'Qu'est-ce que vous voulez que je fasse d'autre?' demanda le poivrot. 'J'suis pas en état de marcher!'

Un ubriaco si avviò barcollando ad una macchina, lascio cadere le chiavi, le raccattò con fatica e provò invano ad infilarne una nella serratura. Un poliziotto gli si avvicinò. 'Non vorrà guidare la macchina in quello stato,' disse. 'E che cosa dovrei fare? Non sono certamente in condizioni di camminare.'

El borracho se acercó a su coche tambaleándose, se le cayeron las llaves, las recogió del suelo y trató en vano de meter una de ellas en la cerradura.
Un policía se le acercó.
—No creerá que está en condiciones de conducir, supongo —le dijo el guardia.
—¿Y qué quiere que haga? —respondió el borracho—. ¡Aún estoy peor para ir andando!

The two drunks leapt into the fountain. After splashing away merrily for a few minutes, one stood up, cupping his hands.
'Guesh wharr I've caught,' he said to his friend.
'An elephan',' said his friend.
'Wrong. Try again.'
'A kangaroo.'
'No. Kangaroosh don' live in water.'
'A mermaid.'
'Right. Ish a mermaid. But wha' kind—blonde or brunette?'

GERMAN

Zwei Betrunkene sprangen in einen Brunnen und planschten fröhlich eine Weile herum. Dann blieb der eine still stehen, schloss die eine Hand leicht über die andere und fragte:
'Raaate mmmmal was ich gefangen habe.'
'Einen Elefanten,' sagte sein Freund.
'Fffalsch. Raaate nnnoch mal.'
'Ein Känguruh.'
'Nee. Känguruhs leben doch nicht im Wasser.'
''Ne Wassernixe.'
'Richtig, 'ne Wassernixe. Blond oder brünett?'

The bricklayer fell from the top of a twelve-storey building, hit a window ledge, bounced off on to some scaffolding, fell from there to the ground, was hit by a passing car and knocked straight through a plate glass window. The foreman rushed over to him, shouting 'Water! Get him water!'
'Water?' groaned the bricklayer. 'What the hell do I have to do for a whisky?'

Ein Maurer stürzt vom 12. Stockwerk des Gebäudes ab, schlägt sofort auf eine Fensterbrüstung auf, prallt ab, fliegt aufs Gerüst, prallt ab und segelt schliesslich durch die Windschutzscheibe eines Autos.
'Wasser! Gebt ihm Wasser!' rief der herbeieilende Aufseher.
'Was habe ich denn falsch gemacht, dass ich keinen Whisky verdiene?' fragt der Maurer stöhnend.

FRENCH

Les deux poivrots plongèrent dans le bassin d'eau. Après s'être amusés comme des petits fous pendant quelques minutes, l'un d'eux se releva, et les mains jointes en forme de coupe, comme s'il tenait quelque chose, il dit à son ami:

'D'vine voir c'qu'j'ai a . . . attrapé?'

'Un éléphant!' répondit l'autre.

'Faux! D'vine encore!'

'Un kangourou.'

'Non! Un kangourou ça vit pas dans l'eau!'

'Une sirène!'

'Bravo! C'est ben une sirène. Mais blonde ou brune?'

ITALIAN

Due ubriachi saltarono nella fontana. Dopo aver sguazzato allegramente per qualche minuto, uno dei due si drizzò in piedi, nascondendo qualche cosa fra le mani.

'Indovina cos'ho preso?' disse.

'Un elefante', rispose l'amico.

'No. Prova un'altra volta.'

'Un canguro.'

'No. I canguri non vivono nell'acqua.'

'Una sirena.'

'Bravo! Proprio una sirena. Ma che tipo? Bionda o bruna?'

SPANISH

Los dos borrachos se metieron en el surtidor. Después de chapotear alegremente unos minutos, uno de ellos se detuvo, haciendo cuenco con las manos.

—¡Adivina lo que he cogido! —le dijo a su amigo.

—Un elefante.

—Te equivocas. Prueba otra vez.

—Un canguro.

—No. Los canguros no viven en el agua.

—Una sirena.

—Exacto. Una sirena. Pero, dime, ¿rubia o morena?

Le maçon tomba du haut du douzième étage d'un immeuble en construction, atterrit sur le rebord d'une fenêtre d'où il rebondit pour aller heurter des éléments d'échafaudage, tomba enfin sur la chaussée mais fut pris en écharpe par une voiture qui l'envoya voltiger à travers la vitrine d'un magasin. Son contremaître se précipita vers lui en criant: 'De l'eau! Donnez lui de l'eaul!' 'De l'eau?' se lamenta ie maçon. 'Après tout ce qui m'est arrivé? Qu'est-ce qu'il faut que je fasse, diable! pour avoir un whisky?'

Un muratore precipitò dalla cima di un palazzo di dodici piani, cascò su di un cornicione, rimbalzò su una impalcatura, di lí cadde a terra, dove fu colpito da una macchina che passava e andò a finire nella vetrina di un negozio, che gli si frantumò addosso. Il capomuratore si precipitò dove il poveretto giaceva, gridando 'Acqua, portategli dell'acqua!'

'Acqua?' gemette il muratore. 'E che diamine devo fare per avere del whisky?'

El albañil se cayó desde lo alto de una casa de doce pisos, pegó en el marco de una ventana, rebotó en un andamio, fué a parar al suelo y un coche que pasaba lo proyectó contra la luna de un escaparate.

El capataz corrió a su lado gritando: —¡Agua! ¡Dadle agua!

—¿Agua? —musitó el albañil—. ¿Qué diantre debo hacer para que me den un vaso de vino?

GERMAN

Walter had married a very beautiful girl. To keep herself looking beautiful she put cream on her face every night and oiled her body all over. This played havoc with Walter's love life. Every time he squeezed her she flew straight through the window.

Walter heiratete ein bildhübsches Mädchen. Nur leider, um schön zu bleiben, balsamierte sie sich jeden Abend von Kopf bis Fuss ein. Und das hatte verheerende Folgen in Walters Liebesleben: sobald er sie in die Arme nahm entschlüpfte sie ihm und flog durchs Fenster.

Jones had discovered his wife making love to another man and had shot her. 'Why,' said the prosecuting counsel at the trial, 'did you shoot your wife and not the other man?'
'I had a choice,' said Jones, 'of shooting a woman once or a different man every week.'

Jones erschoss seine Frau, weil sie ihn mit einem anderen Mann betrog.
'Warum haben Sie Ihre Frau erschossen und nicht den andern Mann?' fragte der Staatsanwalt.
'Dann hätte ich jede Woche einen Mann erschiessen müssen.'

'Do you know what virgins have for breakfast?' said he.
'No,' said she.
'I thought not,' said he.

'Weisst Du, was eine Jungfrau zum Frühstück isst?' fragte er.
'Keine Ahnung,' sagte sie.
'Dachte ich mir doch.'

FRENCH

Walter avait épousé une très belle femme. Celle-ci, pour préserver sa beauté, couvrait tous les soirs son visage de crème et se huilait entièrement le corps. Dans ces conditions, la vie amoureuse de Walter devint un véritable cauchemar; chaque fois qu'il serrait contre lui son épouse, celle-ci lui filait entre les bras comme une anguille pour finir immanquablement à travers la fenêtre.

ITALIAN

Walter aveva sposato una stupenda ragazza. Per mantenersi cosí bella si metteva la crema sulla faccia tutte le notti e si ungeva il corpo con dell'olio. Tale abitudine rese difficile la loro vita coniugale. Ogni volta che Walter la stringeva, la ragazza gli sgusciava tra le mani e finiva fuori dalla finestra.

SPANISH

Walter se casó con una mujer muy guapa. Para conservarse así, todas las noches se ponía crema en la cara y se untaba el cuerpo con aceites. Esto fue causa del fracaso amoroso de Walter. Cada vez que trataba de abrazarla, su mujer salía disparada por la ventana.

Jones avait découvert sa femme au lit avec un autre homme et il l'avait tuée d'un coup de feu.
'Pourquoi,' lui demanda le procureur lors du procès, 'avez-vous tiré sur votre femme et non pas sur son amant?'
'J'avais à choisir,' répondit Jones, 'entre tirer une fois pour toutes sur ma femme ou sur un amant différent chaque semaine.'

Jones aveva scoperto la moglie tra le braccia di un altro uomo, e l'aveva uccisa.
'Perché,' disse l'accusa al processo, 'ha sparato a sua moglie, e non all'uomo?'
'Avevo l'alternativa,' disse Jones, 'tra uccidere una donna una volta per tutte o un uomo diverso ogni settimana.'

Jones sorprendió a su mujer con otro hombre y la mató.
—¿Por qué —le preguntaron durante el juicio— mató usted a su esposa, y no al otro hombre?
—Tenía que elegir —respondió Jones— entre matar una sola mujer o un hombre distinto cada semana.

Lui—'Sais-tu ce que mangent les vierges au petit déjeuner?'
Elle—'Non.'
Lui—'Je m'en doutais bien.'

'Sai che cosa mangiano le vergini alla prima colazione?' chiese lui.
'No,' rispose lei.
'Pensavo che non l'avresti saputo,' disse lui.

—¿Sabes qué toman las vírgenes para desayunar? —dijo él.
—No —dijo ella.
—Ya me lo figuraba —dijo él.

GERMAN

The artist kissed his model tenderly. 'Do you know,' he said, 'you're the first model I've ever made love to?' 'I don't believe it,' she said. 'How many models have you had?' 'Let's see,' said the artist. 'A vase of flowers, a mandolin, a kitten and a bowl of fruit . . .'

Der Maler hielt sein Modell in zärtlicher Umarmung. 'Du bist das erste Modell, mit dem ich ein Liebesverhältnis habe.' 'Das kann ich nicht glauben,' sagte das Mädchen, 'wieviel Modelle hast Du schon gemalt?' 'Warte, lass mich überlegen,' sagte der Maler, 'eine Vase mit Blumen, eine Mandoline, ein Kätzchen, Obst . . .'

Late one night the telephone rang in the police station. 'Send a squad car round to 33 Acacia Avenue—quickly,' said an urgent voice. 'There's a burglar in an old maid's bedroom.' 'Right away,' said the duty sergeant. 'Who's that speaking?' 'The burglar,' said the voice.

Auf der Polizeiwache läutet nachts da Telefon. 'Schicken Sie bitte schnell einen Streifenwagen nach Acacia Avenue 33 . . . da wohnt 'ne alte Jungfer und da ist ein Einbrecher in ihrem Schlafzimmer!' 'Kommen sofort. Und wer spricht da?' 'Der Einbrecher.'

The gay bachelor came back from a fortnight's holiday and immediately asked for another two weeks off to get married. 'But you've just been away for a fortnight,' said the boss: 'Why didn't you get married then?' 'What,' said the bachelor. 'And ruin my holiday?'

Der lustige Junggeselle kommt vom Urlaub zurück und bittet seinen Chef sofort um weitere vierzehn Tage, weil er heiraten will. 'Sie haben doch gerade erst zwei Wochen Urlaub gehabt, warum haben Sie da nicht geheiratet.' 'Weil mir das meinen Urlaub verdorben hätte.'

FRENCH

L'artiste embrassa tendrement son modèle.
'Sais-tu,' lui dit-il, 'que tu es le seul modèle à qui j'aie fait la cour?'
'C'est pas vrai,' dit-elle, 'Combien de modèles tu as eus jusqu'ici?'
'Voyons voir . . .' répond l'artiste, 'un vase de fleurs, une mandoline, un petit chat et une coupe de fruits . . .'

ITALIAN

L'artista baciò teneramente la modella.
'Lo sai,' le disse, 'tu sei la prima modella con la quale ho fatto all'amore.'
'Non ci credo,' rispose lei. 'Quante modelle hai avuto?'
'Vediamo,' replicò l'artista, 'una gattina, una chitarra, delle rose, della frutta. . . .'

SPANISH

El pintor besó tiernamente a su modelo.
—¿Sabes —le dijo— que eres mi primer modelo que me haya enamorado?
—No te creo —dijo ella—. ¿Cuántos modelos has tenido?
—Veamos —respondió el artista—: un jarro de flores, una guitarra, un gatito y un cestillo de frutas . . .

Tard le soir, le téléphone sonne au commissariat de police.
'Vite, une voiture de Police-Secours au 33 Avenue des Acacias,' dit une voix oppressée. 'Il y a un cambrioleur dans la chambre à coucher d'une vieille fille.'
'Tout de suite,' répond l'agent de service. 'Qui êtes-vous?'
'Le cambrioleur,' dit la voix.

A tarda notte il telefono squillò alla stazione di polizia. 'Mandate immediatamente un cellulare al Viale delle Acacie numero 33,' disse una voce ansimante.
'C'è un ladro nella stanza da letto di una vecchia zitella.'
'Subito,' disse l'agente di servizio. 'E chi è che parla?'
'Il ladro,' rispose la voce.

A altas horas de la noche sonó el teléfono en la comisaría.
—¡Manden un coche patrulla a la calle Acacias 33, pronto! —dijo una voz angustiada—. ¡Hay un ladrón en el dormitorio de una vieja criada!
—Está bien —dijo el sargento de guardia—. ¿Quién está al aparato?
—El ladrón —dijo la voz de nuevo.

Le joyeux célibataire rentre de quinze jours de vacances et demande immédiatement deux semaines de congé supplémentaire pour se marier.
'Mais vous venez d'avoir deux semaines de congé,' rétorque le patron, 'pourquoi n'en avez vous pas profité pour vous marier?'
'Quoi?' s'écrie le célibataire, 'et gâcher mes vacances?'

Un allegro scapolo ritornó da due settimane di ferie e immediatamente ne chiese altre due per sposarsi.
'Ma è appena stato via quindici giorni,' disse il capo. 'Perché non si è sposato allora?'
'Già,' rispose lo scapolo, 'cosi avrei rovinato le mie vacanze!'

El alegre soltero regresó de su quincena de vacaciones y en seguida pidió otras dos semanas para casarse.
—Pero si ha estado quince días fuera —le dijo su jefe—, ¿por qué no se casaba entonces?
—¿Y qué —contestó el soltero—. ¿Y arruinar así mis vacaciones?

GERMAN

Never marry for money. You can borrow it much cheaper.

Heirate nie Geld. Borgen ist billiger.

They had made love passionately, but she was still acting coy.
'Tell me, dear,' she said, 'was there anyone else before me?'
The minutes ticked by and there was no answer.
'Darling,' she said, 'I'm still waiting.'
'Just a minute,' he replied, 'I'm still counting.'

Leidenschaftlich lagen sie sich in den Armen und sie spielte noch die Keusche.
'Liebling, waren viele vor mir?'
Schweigen. Die Minuten tickten dahin.
'Liebling,' drängte sie, 'ich warte auf eine Antwort.'
'Moment, ich bin noch beim Zählen.'

'What's the matter, ma'am?' said the maid, finding her mistress in tears.
'I've just discovered that my husband is having an affair with his secretary.'
'Nonsense!' snorted the maid. 'You're only saying that to make me jealous.'

'Ja was ist denn geschehen, gnädige Frau?' fragte das Mädchen als sie die Frau des Hauses in Tränen aufgelöst sah.
'Mein Mann hat ein Verhältnis mit seiner Sekretärin!'
'Ach,' sagte das Mädchen arrogant, 'Sie sagen das nur, um mich eifersüchtig zu machen.'

Most married men tell lies for only one reason: their wives' questions.

Die meisten Männer lügen nur, weil ihre Frauen zu viel fragen.

FRENCH	ITALIAN	SPANISH
Ne jamais se marier pour de l'argent. On peut l'emprunter moins cher.	Non sposarti per denaro. È molto piú economico prenderlo in prestito.	No te cases por dinero. Sale más a cuenta pedirlo prestado.
Ils venaient de faire passionnément l'amour, mais elle demeurait cependant comme timidement gênée. 'Dis moi, chéri,' demanda-t-elle, 'tu as connu beaucoup de filles avant moi?' De longues minutes se passent sans aucune réponse. 'Chéri,' dit-elle, 'j'attends.' 'Un instant, veux-tu,' répondit-il, 'je suis en train de compter.'	Avevano fatto appassionatamente all'amore, ma lei faceva ancora la modestina. 'Dimmi, caro,' gli chiese 'ce ne sono state altre prima di me?' I minuti passavano e lui non rispondeva. 'Tesoro,' disse lei, 'sto ancora aspettando.' 'Un momento,' rispose lui, 'sto ancora contando.'	Se habían hecho el amor apasionadamente, pero ella parecía aun algo remisa. —Dime querido —dijo—. ¿Hubo otra mujer antes que yo? Pasaron algunos minutos y la respuesta no llegaba. —Querido —insistió—. Todavía estoy esperando. —Un momento . . . —respuso él—. Es que las estoy contando.
'Qu'y a-t-il, Madame?' demanda la servante à sa maîtresse en pleurs. 'Je viens de découvrir à l'instant que mon mari me trompe avec sa secrétaire.' 'A d'autres!' répliqua la servante, 'vous dites ça pour me rendre jalouse.'	'Che cosa c'è, signora?' chiese la cameriera trovando la padrona in lacrime. 'Ho appena scoperto che mio marito se la vede con la segretaria.' 'Sciocchezze!' sbofonchió la cameriera. 'Lo dice solo per rendermi gelosa.'	—¿Qué le pasa, señora —dijo la doncella al encontrar a su ama anegada en llanto. —Acabo de descubrir que mi marido me engaña con su secretaria. —¡Tonterías! —exclamó la criada—. ¡Eso lo dice para darme celos!
La plupart des maris ne mentent que parce que leurs femmes posent des questions.	Gli unici motivi che inducono a mentire la maggior parte degli uomini: le domande delle mogli.	La mayoría de los hombres mienten por una sola razón: por las preguntas de sus esposas.

GERMAN

'Excuse me, sir,' said the clerk, 'but I'd like to have a day off to attend my mother-in-law's funeral.'
'So would I,' said his boss, 'but the old bag just won't die.'

'Herr Direktor, ich hätte gern einen Tag frei, um dem Begräbnis meiner Schwiegermutter beizuwohnen.'
'Ich auch, aber die Alte stirbt nie!'

The business man arrived home in the early hours of the morning after a busy night with his secretary.
All went well until his wife woke up as he was undressing.
'Alfred!' she exclaimed: 'Where's your underwear?'
'Dear me,' he said, thinking quickly, 'I've been robbed!'

Der Ehemann kam sehr spät nach einer arbeitsreichen Nacht mit seiner Sekretärin nach Haus. Er zog sich ganz leise aus, aber plötzlich wachte seine Frau doch auf.
'Alfred,' rief sie, 'wo ist denn Deine Unterwäsche?'
'Himmel,' rief Alfred, 'die hat jemand geklaut!'

Now that women wear false eyelashes, false bosoms and false hair, a man doesn't stand a chance. A friend of ours once followed a girl for three miles—and then found it was his mother.

Heute tragen Frauen falsche Wimperm, falsche Busen, falsche Haare und ein Mann weiss nicht mehr woran er ist.
Mein Freund ist einem Mädchen eine ganze Stunde nachgestiegen und dann war es seine Mutter.

FRENCH	ITALIAN	SPANISH
'Excusez-moi, Monsieur,' dit l'employé, 'mais je voudrais prendre un jour de congé pour l'enterrement de ma belle-mère.' 'Et moi pareillement,' répond le patron, 'l'ennui, c'est que cette vieille rosse ne se décide pas à crever!'	'Mi scusi signore,' disse l'impiegato, 'vorrei un giorno libero per andare ai funerali di mia suocera.' 'Anch'io lo vorrei,' rispose il principale, 'ma quella vecchia befana non muore mai.'	—Perdone, señor —dijo el empleado—. Quisiera pedirle un día libre para asistir a los funerales de mi suegra. —¡Eso quisiera yo también! —contestó el dueño— Pero la vieja no acaba nunca de morirse.
L'homme d'affaires rentre chez lui à l'aube après une nuit assez agitée dans le lit de sa secrétaire. Tout se passe bien jusqu'au moment où sa femme se réveille alors qu'il est en train de se déshabiller. 'Alfred!' s'écrie-t-elle, 'où sont passés tes sous-vêtements?' 'Grands Dieux!' dit-il, tâchant de réfléchir vite, 'on m'a volé!'	Un uomo d'affari tornò a casa nelle ore piccole, dopo aver passato la notte con la segretaria. Tutto ando bene, finché la moglie non si svegliò proprio mentre lui si stava spogliando. 'Alfredo,' esclamò, 'dov'è la tua biancheria intima?' 'Oh povero me' disse lui con prontezza di spirito, 'sono stato derubato.'	El hombre de negocios vuelve a su casa de madrugada, después de una noche muy ocupada con su secretaria. Todo iba bien, hasta que su mujer se despertó mientras se desnudaba. —¡Alfredo! —exclamó—. ¿Dónde está la ropa interior? —Verás, querida . . . —respondió precipitadamente—. ¡Me han robado!
Maintenant que les femmes portent de faux-cils, de faux-seins et des perruques, les hommes n'ont plus aucune chance de s'y retrouver. Un de nos amis a suivi un jour une femme pendant cinq kilomètres, avant de s'apercevoir que c'était sa propre mère qu'il suivait.	Ora che le donne portano ciglia finte, seni finti e capelli finti, all'uomo non ne va piú bene una. Un nostro amico una volta seguí una ragazza per cinque chilometri—e poi scoperse che era sua madre.	Ahora que las mujeres llevan pestañas postizas, pechos postizos y pelo postizo, los hombres tienen pocas posibilidades. Un amigo mío siguió en una ocasión a una chica más de tres kilómetros, y al final descubrió que era su madre.

GERMAN

The fastest worker we ever knew was a man who rushed up to a girl and said: 'I'm a stranger in town. Direct me to your flat.'

Der schlimmste Draufgänger war der Mann, der ein Mädchen ansprach und sagte:
'Verzeihen Sie bitte, ich bin fremd hier, können Sie mir den Weg in Ihre Wohnung zeigen?'

'I'm afraid your new baby is a bit on the small side, Mrs Jones,' said the doctor. 'It only weighs a pound and a half.'
'What else could you expect, doctor?' said Mrs Jones. 'I've only been married six weeks.'

'Leider ist Ihr Baby sehr klein, Mrs Jones,' sagte der Arzt.
'Es wiegt nur anderthalb Pfund.'
'Mehr kann man ja auch nicht erwarten, Herr Doktor, ich bin ja auch erst seit sechs Wochen verheiratet.'

'Do you ever talk to your wife while you're making love?'
'Only if there's a 'phone by the bed.'

'Sprichst Du mit Deiner Frau im Liebesrausch?'
'Ja, wenn ein Telefon am Bett ist.'

The biggest problem in a bachelor's life is how to explain it to his son.

Das grösste Problem für einen Junggesellen ist: 'Wie sag' ich's meinem Sohne.'

FRENCH	ITALIAN	SPANISH
J'en ai connu des gars rapides qui vous baratinent une fille en cinq secs; mais le champion c'est le type qui s'est précipité un jour vers une fille et lui a dit: 'J'suis pas d'ici. Montre moi vite ton chez toi.'	L'uomo piú svelto di nostra conoscenza è uno che si precipitò verso una ragazza e disse: 'Sono nuovo del luogo, mi può indicare come arrivare al suo appartamento?'	El hombre más rápido que he conocido fué uno que se acercó a una chica y le dijo: —Soy forastero en la ciudad. Llévame a tu piso.
'J'ai bien peur que votre nouveau-né ne soit un peu petit, Mme Jones,' dit le docteur. 'Il pèse à peine une livre et demie.' 'Mais enfin, docteur, à quoi vous attendiez-vous?' répliqua Mme Jones, 'je ne suis mariée que depuis un mois et demi!'	'Mi spiace dirle che il neonato è un po' piccolino, Signora Jones,' disse il dottore alla puerpera, 'pesa solo 800 grammi.' 'Che cosa potevamo aspettarci, Dottore?' disse la Signora Jones. 'Sono sposata solo da sei settimane.'	Siento decirle que su hijo es más bien algo pequeño, señora Jones —dijo el médico—. Sólo pesa una libra y media. —¿Y qué esperaba, doctor? —repuso la señora Jones—. ¡Sólo llevo seis semanas de casada!
'Est-ce qu'il vous arrive jamais de parler à votre femme en faisant l'amour?' 'Seulement s'il y a un téléphone près du lit.'	'Parli mai a tua moglie mentre fai all'amore?' 'Solo se c'è un telefono vicino al letto.'	—¿Hablas siempre con tu esposa mientras haces el amor? —Sólo si hay un teléfono junto a la cama.
Pour un célibataire le plus gros problème dans sa vie c'est d'expliquer la situation à son fils.	Il problema piú grosso della vita di uno scapolo è come spiegarla al proprio figlio.	El mayor problema en la vida de un soltero es cómo explicarle eso a su hijo.

GERMAN

The widow brought a faded old picture of her late husband into the photographer's.
'Could you enlarge this for me?'
'Certainly, madam.'
'And could you remove his hat?'
'Certainly, madam. Could you tell me on which side his hair was parted?'
'After all these years I can't remember—but surely you'll find out when you take his hat off.'

Die Witwe gab dem Fotografen ein verblasstes Foto von ihrem verstorbenen Mann.
'Können Sie das vergrössern?'
'Gewiss, gnädige Frau.'
'Ohne Hut?'
'Selbstverständlich. Sie müssen mir nur sagen, auf welcher Seite Ihr Gatte den Scheitel hatte.'
'Das weiss ich nach den vielen Jahren nicht mehr—aber Sie werden es ja sehen, wenn Sie den Hut abnehmen.'

Cyril was not the brightest of men. One day he turned up at the office in a smart new suit.
'A present from the wife,' he said proudly.
'Was it a surprise?' said his friend.
'A complete surprise,' said Cyril. 'I got home early yesterday and there it was, lying on the bed.'

Sehr gescheit war Cyril nicht.
Eines Tages kommt er ins Büro in einem sehr eleganten Anzug.
'Ein Geschenk von meiner Frau,' sagte er stolz.
'War es eine Überraschung?' fragte sein Freund.
'Eine völlige Überraschung. Ich kam gestern etwas früher nach Haus und da lag er—ausgebreitet auf dem Bett.'

Many a man takes the first step towards divorce—by getting married.

Für viele Männer ist der erste Schritt zur Scheidung—die Hochzeit.

FRENCH	ITALIAN	SPANISH
Une veuve apporte au photographe une vieille photo jaunie de son défunt époux. 'Pouvez-vous m'en faire un agrandissement?' 'Certainement, Madame.' 'Et pouvez-vous aussi lui enlever le chapeau?' 'Mais certainement, Madame. Pourriez-vous me dire de quel côté il portait la raie?' 'Il y a si longtemps, je ne m'en souviens plus . . . Mais vous le verrez sûrement lorsque vous lui enlèverez le chapeau!'	La vedova portò dal fotografo una vecchia istantanea sbiadita del marito defunto. 'Me ne potrebbe fare un ingrandimento?' 'Certo, signora.' 'E potrebbe togliergli il cappello?' 'Certo, signora. Mi può dire da che parte aveva la scriminatura dei capelli?' 'Dopo tutti questi anni, non me lo ricordo. Ma quando gli avrà tolto il cappello, potrà vederlo da sé.'	La viuda llevó una foto amarillenta de su último marido a casa del fotógrafo. —¿Podría sacarme una ampliación? —Ya lo creo, señora. —¿Y podría quitarle el sombrero? —Desde luego, señora. Dígame tan sólo a qué lado de la cabeza llevaba la raya. —Verá, después de tantos años ya no me acuerdo. Pero eso lo sabrá en seguida, en cuanto le quite el sombrero.
Côté intellect, Cyril n'était pas un génie. Un jour, il arriva au bureau vêtu d'un élégant costume tout neuf. 'Un cadeau de ma femme,' annonça-t-il fièrement. 'Tu t'y attendais?' demanda un de ses amis. 'Pas le moins du monde,' répondit Cyril, 'une surprise totale. Figure-toi que je suis rentré assez tôt chez moi, hier, et que vois-je? Ce même costume étalé sur le lit!'	Cyril non brillava per la sua intelligenza. Un giorno arrivò in ufficio con un elegante vestito nuovo. 'Un regalo di mia moglie,' disse tutto fiero. 'È stata una sorpresa?' gli chiese un amico. 'Una vera sorpresa', rispose Cyril. 'Sono arrivato a casa presto ieri, ed era lí, disteso sul letto.'	Cirilo no es lo que diríamos un tipo listo. Un día se presentó en la oficina con un traje nuevo. —Un regalo de mi mujer —dijo con orgullo. —¿Ha sido una sorpresa? —le preguntó un compañero. —¡Una completa sorpresa! —añadió Cirilo—. Ayer llegué a casa temprano, y allí estaba el traje, encima de la cama.
C'est bien en se mariant que beaucoup ont franchi le premier pas vers le divorce.	Molti uomini fanno il primo passo verso il divorzio il giorno delle proprie nozze.	Muchos hombres dan el primer paso hacia el divorcio . . . casándose.

The manager of the local store rang up Mr Smith.
'It's about your wife,' he said hesitantly. 'She has been coming in here for the past week, buying all sorts of things, and offering to pay in milk-bottle tops. I've humoured her so far, because she's always been a good customer, but it's getting rather worrying.'
'It's quite all right,' said Mr Smith. 'She's not been quite herself lately. Just let her have whatever she wants and I'll come in and settle the bill at the end of the month.'
The manager agreed. For the rest of the month Mrs Smith came in the store, bought mountains of goods, and was allowed to pay in milk-bottle tops. Mr Smith turned up on the appointed day to pay for everything.
'How much?' he asked.
'£144. 19s. 6d.,' said the manager.
'That's fine,' said Mr Smith. 'Do you have change for this dustbin lid?'

GERMAN

Der Manager vom Kaufhaus ruft Mr Smith an.
'Es ist wegen Ihrer Frau, Mr Smith. Sie machte in dieser Woche sehr viele Einkäufe, die sie alle mit Milchflaschendeckel bezahlte. Ich habe die Sache bisher von der humoristischen Seite gesehen; schliesslich ist sie ja immer eine gute Kundin gewesen. Aber ich mache mir doch langsam Gedanken.'
'Das geht in Ordnung, sagte Mr Smith. 'Meine Frau war nicht so ganz in Ordnung in der letzten Zeit, aber geben Sie ihr nur, was sie haben will; ich komme Ende des Monats und begleiche alles.'
Der Manager war zufrieden und Mrs Smith durfte mit ihren Flaschendeckeln kaufen was sie wollte.
Am Monatsende erschien Mr Smith, wie verabredet.
'Also, was schulde ich Ihnen?'
'Hundertachtundzanzig Mark und dreissig Pfennig.'
Sicher wie ein Mann, der sich um Haushaltssorgen zu kümmern versteht, legte er dem erstaunten Manager einen nagelneuen Mülleimerdeckel auf den Schreibtisch, und sagte zufrieden: 'Dann bekomme ich ja noch einige Milchdeckel zurück.'

FRENCH

Le gérant du magasin téléphone à M. Smith.
'C'est au sujet de votre femme,' explique-t-il un peu gêné, 'Voilà une semaine qu'elle vient chez nous pour acheter toutes sortes de choses, et elle nous donne à titre de paiement des capsules de bouteilles de lait. J'ai bien voulu marcher, jusqu'à présent, parce qu'elle a toujours été une bonne cliente, mais cela commence à m'inquiéter un peu.'
'Ne vous tracassez pas,' dit M. Smith. 'Il est vrai qu'elle n'est plus du tout la même depuis quelque temps. Laissez-la prendre tout ce qu'elle veut et je passerai moi-même vous régler à la fin du mois.'
Le gérant est d'accord et pendant tout le restant du mois, Mme Smith arrive au magasin, achète des tonnes de marchandises qu'elle paie avec des capsules de bouteilles de lait.
La fin du mois arrive et le jour dit M. Smith arrive au magasin pour payer toute la facture. 'Combien?' demande-t-il.
'£144. 19*s.* 6*d.*,' déclare le gérant.
'Parfait,' répond M. Smith, 'Pouvez-vous me faire la monnaie de ce couvercle de poubelle?'

ITALIAN

Il direttore di un grande magazzino telefonò al Signor Smith.
'Volevo parlarle riguardo a sua moglie,' disse imbarazzato, 'sa, sono diversi giorni che viene nel mio negozio, compra un sacco di cose ed offre di pagare con i tappi delle bottiglie del latte. Fino adesso sono stato al giuoco, perché si tratta di una buona cliente, ma adesso la cosa comincia a preoccuparmi . . .'
'Non si dia pensiero,' disse il Signor Smith, 'sa, da un po' di tempo mia moglie non è stata proprio bene . . . Le dia pure tutto quello che vuole, e poi passerò io stesso a saldare il conto alla fine del mese.'
Il direttore disse che era d'accordo. Durante il resto del mese la Signora Smith continuò ad arrivare al negozio, a comprare un sacco di cose, e a pagare con i tappi delle bottiglie del latte.
Il Signor Smith si presentò all'ultimo del mese, come pattuito.
'Quanto devo?' domando.
'Centoquarantaquattro sterline,' disse il direttore.
'Bene,' disse il Signor Smith, 'mi può dare il resto a questo coperchio di pattumiera?'

SPANISH

El director de los grandes almacenes telefonea al señor Smith.
—Se trata de su esposa . . . —dice con aire de duda—. Viene por aquí desde hace unas semanas, adquiere toda clase de objetos y pretende pagar con chapas de leche embotellada. Hasta ahora le he seguido la broma porque siempre ha sido una buena cliente, pero ya empieza a preocuparme . . .
—No haga caso —le responde el señor Smith—. Hace un tiempo que no está muy bien, ¿sabe? Déle usted lo que pida, y yo pasaré a liquidar la cuenta a final de mes.
El director accedió. Durante los días restantes, la señora Smith iba a la tienda, compraba montañas de géneros y pagaba con chapas de botella.
El día convenido, el señor Smith fué a pagar el importe de las compras.
—¿Cuánto es? —preguntó'
—144 libras, 19 chelines y 6 peniques —contestó el director.
—De acuerdo —repuso el señor Smith—. ¿Tendrá cambio de esta tapadera del cubo de la basura?

GERMAN

Adam was lucky. Eve could never nag him about all the other men she could have married.

Adam hatte ein Glück! Eva konnte ihm nichts von ihren verpassten Chancen mit anderen Männern vorjammern.

'Did you sleep with my wife?' demanded the jealous husband.
'Not a wink,' said the gigolo, 'not a wink.'

'Haben Sie mit meiner Frau geschlafen?' fragte der eifersüchtige Ehemann erregt.
'Nicht eine Sekunde,' sagte der Gigolo.

Henry was getting married next day. Over a drink at the bachelor party, his father gave him some sound advice: 'Always insist on having a night out with the boys. And don't waste it on the boys.'

Auf der Junggesellenparty am Abend vor Harrys Hochzeit gibt ihm der Vater noch ein paar gute Ratschläge.
'Du musst gleich darauf bestehen, dass Du einen Abend in der Woche mit Deinen Freunden verbringen kannst. Aber verbringe den Abend dann nicht etwa mit Deinen Freunden.'

FRENCH	ITALIAN	SPANISH
Adam. En voilà un qui avait de la chance! Eve ne pouvait jamais l'enquiquiner en lui parlant de tous les autres hommes qu'elle aurait pu épouser.	Adamo era un uomo fortunato. Eva non poteva tormentarlo con tutti gli uomini che avrebbe potuto sposare.	Adán tuvo suerte. Eva nunco le mortificó hablándole de los hombres con que hubiera podido casarse.
'Alors, on a fait dodo avec ma femme?' demanda le mari jaloux. 'Pas du tout! Avec elle, y a pas moyen de fermer l'œil!'	'Hai dormito con mia moglie?' domandò il marito geloso. 'Macché,' rispose il gigoló, 'non ho potuto chiudere occhio.'	—¿Ha dormido usted con mi esposa? —le preguntó el marido celoso. —¡Ni siquiera una siestecita! —respondió el gigoló—. ¡Ni siquiera una siestecita!
Henry se mariait le jour suivant. A la soirée qu'il avait organisée pour enterrer sa vie de garçon, son père, entre deux verres, lui donne quelques bons conseils: 'Ne te laisse pas faire; insiste toujours pour avoir une soirée à toi que tu passeras avec les copains. Mais ne va pas la gaspiller précisément avec les copains!'	Henry si doveva sposare all'indomani. Durante un ricevimento per dare l'addio al celibato, suo padre gli offrí dei buoni consigli, 'Devi sempre insistere per passare una serata solo con gli amici. E non sprecarla con gli amici!'	Enrique iba a casarse al día siguiente. Después de unos tragos en la despedida de soltero, su padre le dió un prudente consejo: —Insiste siempre en disponer de una noche para los amigos. Pero no la malgastes saliendo con ellos.

GERMAN

My wife's thirty-fifth isn't far away. It was just five years ago.	Der fünfunddreissigste Geburtstag meiner Frau ist nicht fern—nur erst fünf Jahre her.
I AM NOT SAYING MY WIFE IS FAT BUT . . . If she falls down she rocks herself to sleep trying to get up.	ICH WILL MEINE FRAU NICHT FETT NENNEN, ABER . . . wenn sie hinfällt, rollt sie sich beim Wiederaufstehen in den Schlaf.
She can answer a knock at the front door without leaving the kitchen.	wenn es klopft, kann sie zur Wohnungstür gehen, ohne die Küche zu verlassen.
The only time she rode a camel, the hump finished up underneath.	als sie sich einmal auf ein Dromedar setzte, hat sie den Höcker nacht unten durchgedrückt.
When I make love to her I have to use a chalk and a piece of string to make sure I've covered everything. The other night I found a little man coming round the other way.	ein Liebesspiel mit ihr wird zur Vermessungskunst. Neulich kam mir beim Feldmessen ein kleiner Mann aus der anderen Richtung entgegen.
When she has a shower it takes her half an hour to get her feet wet.	es dauert eine halbe Stunde bis ihre Füsse beim Duschen nass werden.

FRENCH	ITALIAN	SPANISH
Le trente-cinquième anniversaire de ma femme n'est pas très loin. Il y a juste cinq ans, c'est tout!	Mia moglie non è molto lontana dal suo trentacinquesimo compleanno. L'ha compiuto solo cinque anni fa.	Mi esposa está cerca de los treinta y cinco. Los cumplió hace sólo cinco años.
JE N'IRAIS PAS JUSQU'A DIRE QUE MA FEMME SOIT GROSSE, MAIS . . . S'il lui arrive de tomber, elle finit par se bercer et s'endormir à force de basculer d'un côté à l'autre en essayant de se relever.	NON CHE MIA MOGLIE SIA GRASSA MA . . . Se cade bisogna trovare degli argani per rimetterla in piedi.	YO NO DIGO QUE MI MUJER SEA GORDA, PERO . . . Si se cae, se queda dormida tratando de levantarse.
Elle peut répondre à un coup de sonnette à la porte d'entrée sans avoir à sortir de la cuisine.	Se qualcuno bussa alla porta di casa può aprirla senza uscire dalla cucina.	Puede atender una llamada en la puerta principal sin salir de la cocina.
La seule fois où elle est montée sur un chameau, la pauvre bête a eu sa bosse complètement raplatie.	L'unica volta che andò in sella ad un cammello la gobba del povero animale quasi toccò terra.	La única vez que montó un camello, la joroba le salió por abajo.
Lorsque je lui fais l'amour, il me faut de la craie et de la ficelle pour marquer mes points de repère. L'autre soir, par exemple, je me suis trouvé nez à nez avec un petit bonhomme qui lui remontait le flanc de l'autre côté.	Quando facciamo all'amore devo servirmi di un pezzo di gesso e uno spago per essere sicuro di aver coperto tutto il territorio. L'altra notte incontrai un ometto che avanzava in direzione opposta.	Cuando me acuesto con ella tengo que usar una tiza y un cordel para estar seguro de haberlo explorado todo. La otra noche encontré a un hombrecillo que aparecía por el otro lado.
Lorsqu'elle se douche, il faut une demi-heure avant que l'eau lui arrive aux pieds.	Quando fa la doccia ci vuole mezz'ora prima che riesca a bagnarsi i piedi.	Cuando se ducha, necesita media hora para mojarse los pies.

	GERMAN
My wife's hats never go out of fashion. They look just as ridiculous every year.	Die Hüte meiner Frau werden nie altmodisch—sie sehen jedes Jahr unmöglich aus.
I wouldn't say my wife has a big mouth, but she's the only woman I know who can eat a cucumber sideways.	Ich will ja nichts behaupten, aber nur meine Frau kann lange grüne Gurken horizontal essen.
For years my wife and I were deliriously happy. Then we met.	Jahrelang waren meine Frau und ich so glücklich. Dann trafen wir uns.
I married the girl of my dreams. Ever since she's been a nightmare.	Meine Frau war das Mädchen meiner Träume; jetzt ist sie mein Alptraum.
My wife is so ugly that at our wedding everybody kissed the bridesmaid.	Meine Frau ist so hässlich, dass auf unserer Hochzeit jeder die Brautjungfer geküsst hat.
My wife is celebrating the fifteenth anniversary of her twenty-fifth birthday.	Meine Frau feiert jetzt den fünfzehnten Jahrestag ihres fünfundzwanzigsten Geburtstags.

FRENCH	ITALIAN	SPANISH
Les chapeaux de ma femme ne sont jamais démodés. D'une année à l'autre, le ridicule ne les quitte pas.	I cappellini di mia moglie non sono mai fuori moda. Continuano ad essere ridicoli anno dopo anno.	Los sombreros de mi mujer nunca pasan de moda. Son igual de ridículos cada año.
Je n'irais pas jusqu'à dire que ma femme a une grande bouche, mais c'est la seule personne que je connaisse qui puisse manger un concombre de travers.	Non dico che mia moglie abbia la bocca grande, ma è l'unica donna che conosco che riesce a mangiare un cetriolo per il verso orizzontale.	Yo no digo que mi mujer tenga la boca grande, pero es la única que conozco, capaz de comerse un pepino puesto de lado.
Pendant des années et des années, ma femme et moi avons été terriblement heureux... jusqu'au jour oû nous nous sommes rencontrés.	Per anni mia moglie e io siamo stati pazzamente felici. Poi ci incontrammo.	Durante muchos años mi mujer y yo fuimos muy felices. Luego, nos conocimos.
J'ai épousé la jeune fille de mes rêves. Depuis, c'est un véritable cauchemar.	Ho sposato la donna dei miei sogni. Da allora è diventata un incubo.	Me casé con la mujer de mis sueños. Desde entonces se convirtió en una pesadilla.
Ma femme est si laide que le jour du mariage tout le monde a embrassé la demoiselle d'honneur.	Mia moglie è cosí brutta che al nostro matrimonio gli amici hanno baciato la damigella d'onore.	Mi mujer es tan fea que el día de nuestra boda todos besaron a la madrina.
Ma femme fête le quinzième anniversaire de ses vingt-cinq ans.	Mia moglie sta per celebrare il quindicesimo anniversario del suo venticinquesimo compleanno.	Mi mujer celebra el décimoquinto aniversario de su veinticinco cumpleaños.

GERMAN

When my wife sang in the church choir, half the congregation changed their religion.

Als meine Frau im Kirchenchor gesungen hat, wechselte die Hälfte der Gemeinde den Glauben.

My marriage is a real love story. I love my wife and so does she.

Meine Ehe ist eine wahre Liebesgeschichte: ich liebe meine Frau—und sie auch.

My wife doesn't need a washing machine. She married one.

Meine Frau braucht keine Waschmachine—sie hat eine geheiratet.

My wife is so fat that every time she stands on a speak-your-weight machine it shouts 'Get off!'

So dick ist meine Frau, dass jede gewichtansagende Waage 'RUNTER!' schreit, sobald sie sich draufstellt.

My wife had an hour-glass figure. Then all the sand shifted to the bottom.

Meine Frau hatte eine Eieruhrfigur—bis sich der Sand unten festgesetzt hat.

My wife once put on a mudpack. It improved her appearance tremendously for a while. Then she took it off.

Meine Frau hatte sich eine Schlammpackung aufgelegt, die sie sofort viel aübscher machte. Sie wusch sie leider wieder ab.

FRENCH	ITALIAN	SPANISH
Lorsqu'elle a chanté pour la première fois à l'église, ma femme a amené la moitié des fidèles à changer de religion.	Quando mia moglie cantò nel coro della chiesa, metà dei fedeli decise di convertirsi.	Cuando mi mujer cantó en el coro de la iglesia, la mitad de los fieles cambiaron de religión.
Mon mariage est une véritable histoire d'amour. J'aime ma femme et elle s'aime beaucoup.	Il mio matrimonio è una vera storia d'amore. Io amo mia moglie, e lei ama se stessa.	Mi matrimonio es una verdadera historia de amor. Yo amo a mi mujer y ella hace lo mismo.
Ma femme n'a pas besoin d'une machine à laver. Elle en a épousé une.	Mia moglie non ha bisogno di una lavatrice. Ne ha sposata una.	Mi mujer no necesita una lavadora. Se casó con una.
Ma femme est si grosse que chaque fois qu'elle se pèse sur une bascule parlante celle-ci lui hurle: 'Tire-toi d'là!'	Mia moglie è talmente grassa che ogni volta che monta su una bilancia parlante la macchina urla: 'Scenda!'	Mi mujer es tan gorda que cuando se sube a una báscula autoparlante, ésta se pone a gritar: '¡Bájate de ahí!'
Ma femme avait une taille fine comme celle d'un sablier. Puis un jour, tout le sable a dégringolé vers le bas.	Mia moglie aveva la silhouette di una clessidra. Poi tutta la sabbia è scesa giú.	Mi mujer tenía la silueta de un reloj de arena. Pero todo el contenido se le ha ido para abajo.
Un jour, ma femme a décidé de se mettre sur le visage un emplâtre de boues. C'est fou ce que cela l'a embellie. Puis, malheureusement, elle l'a enlevé.	Una volta mia moglie si fece una maschera di fango. Per un po' migliorò molto il suo aspetto. Purtroppo se la tolse.	Mi mujer se puso una vez un corsé. De momento mejoró notablemente su apariencia. Pero luego se lo quitó.

	GERMAN
My parents mustn't have been expecting me. The day after I was born they left home.	Meine Eltern haben mich bestimmt nicht erwartet. Sie sind am nächsten Tag ausgezogen.
When I was born my mother said: 'O.K. The joke's over—now bring me the baby.'	Als ich geboren wurde, sagte meine Mutter: 'Also nun Spass beiseite—wo ist das Baby.'
I was born at home. But when mother saw me she had to be taken to hospital.	Ich bin zuhaus geboren. Als mich meine Mutter sah, musste man sie sofort ins Krankenhaus bringen.
My mother didn't call me nasty names like everyone else did—she just didn't speak to me.	Meine Mutter hat mir nie Gemeinheiten an den Kopf geworfen wie alle andern; sie hat nie mit mir gesprochen.
After I was born my father took up a new hobby—shooting storks.	Als ich geboren wurde, hat sich mein Vater sofort ein neues Steckenpferd zugelegt: Storchjagd.
My father was very fond of me. He used to give me all his old razor blades to play with.	Mein Vater war immer sehr nett zu mir. Ich durfte auch immer mit seinen gebrauchten Rasierklingen spielen.

FRENCH	ITALIAN	SPANISH
Il faut croire que mes parents ne s'attendaient guère à moi. Le lendemain de ma naissance, ils ont fichu le camp.	I miei genitori non dovevano aspettarsi la mia nascita. Il giorno dopo il mio arrivo se ne andarono di casa.	Mis padres no debían esperarme. Al día siguiente de nacer yo se marcharon de casa.
Le jour de ma naissance, ma mère a dit: 'Bon. Finie la plaisanterie, passe moi le bébé maintenant.'	Quando nacqui mia madre esclamò: 'Va bene, basta con gli scherzi. Adesso portatemi il neonato.'	Cuando yo nací, mi madre dijo: —¡Bueno, el cuento ha terminado; ahora tráeme al niño!
Je suis né à la maison. Mais quand elle m'a vu, ma mère a dû être transportée à l'hôpital.	Sono nato a casa. Ma quando mia madre mi vide dovettero portarla all'ospedale.	Yo nací en casa. Pero cuando mi madre me vió, tuvieron que llevarla al hospital.
Ma mère ne m'a pas traité de tous les noms comme tout le monde; elle a simplement refusé de m'adresser la parole.	Mia madre non mi chiamò mai con i brutti nomi che usavano tutti gli altri—semplicemente non mi rivolse la parola.	Mi madre no me dijo las palabrotas que cualquiera me hubiera dicho. Simplemente, no me dirigió la palabra.
Après ma naissance, mon père s'est décidé à prendre un nouveau passe-temps: la chasse au cigognes.	Dopo la mia nascita mio padre si dedicò a un nuovo sport: la caccia alla cicogna.	Al nacer yo, mi padre se buscó una nueva distracción: matar cigüeñas.
Mon père avait beaucoup d'affection pour moi. Il me donnait toutes ses vieilles lames de rasoir pour jouer avec.	Mio padre non mi voleva molto bene. Mi dava tutte le sue lamette usate da giocare.	Mi padre era muy cariñoso conmigo. Siempre me daba sus hojas de afeitar usadas para jugar con ellas.

THE DEAR OLD LADY

GERMAN

The dear old lady had never been out of her village before, so her relatives took her into the big city for a treat.
On her return she was telling her friends all about it—especially about her visit to the zoo, where she had been impressed by the elephant.
'This great big animal,' she said, 'was picking up buns with its tail. I don't dare tell you what it did with them.'

Das alte Mütterchen war nie aus ihrem Dorf herausgekommen; deshalb machten ihr ihre Verwandten eine besondere Freude mit einem Ausflug in die Stadt.
Nach ihrer Rückkehr erzählte sie ihren Freunden von ihren Erlebnissen—besonders über ihren Besuch im Zoo, wo ein Elefant sie sehr beeindruckt hatte.
'Dieses Riesentier hob mit seinem Schwanz Brötchen auf,' berichtete sie, 'aber ich kann es Euch unmöglich sagen, was er dann damit gemacht hat!'

The old lady had been worrying the life out of the captain all through the voyage.
When the ship docked, he said to her: 'You can stop worrying now, madam. We've dropped the anchor.'
'I'm not surprised,' said the old lady. 'It's been hanging over the side for days.'

Die alte Dame ging dem Kapitän mit ihrer Ängstlichkeit während der ganzen Reise auf die Nerven.
Als das Schiff anlegte, sagte er zu ihr: 'Jetzt brauchen Sie sich keine Sorgen mehr zu machen, der Anker ist unten.'
'Das überrascht mich gar nicht,' sagt die alte Dame, 'wenn Sie den draussen hängen lassen.'

'Do your planes crash very often?' said the nervous old lady to the pilot.
'No, madam. Only once.'

'Stürzen Ihre Flugzeuge oft ab?' fragte die alte Dame nervös den Piloten.
'Nein, gnädige Frau, nur einmal.'

FRENCH

La bonne petite vieille dame n'avait jamais quitté son village; aussi ses parents décidèrent de l'emmener visiter la capitale pour lui faire plaisir.
A son retour, elle raconta à toutes ses amies ce qu'elle avait vu, surtout lors de sa visite au zoo où elle avait été particulièrement impressionné par l'éléphant.
'Cette grosse bête,' dit-elle, 'prenait les gâteaux avec sa queue. Je n'ose pas vous dire ce qu'elle en faisait!'

ITALIAN

La brava vecchietta in vita sua non era mai stata fuori dal suo villaggio. I parenti un giorno decisero di farle vedere la grande città.
Al ritorno la vecchietta raccontò alle amiche tutto ciò che aveva fatto e si soffermò in particolar modo sulla visita allo zoo, dove piú di tutto le aveva fatto impressione l'elefante.
'Questo gigantesco animale,' spiegò, 'prendeva le brioches con la coda. Non oso precisare cosa ne facesse in seguito.'

SPANISH

La viejecita no había salido nunca de su pueblo hasta que sus familiares la invitaron a pasar unos días en la gran ciudad.
A su regreso contaba a sus amistades todo lo que había visto, particularmente en el zoológico, donde lo que más le impresionó fue el elefante.
—Este animal tan grandote —decía—, iba recogiendo los panecillos con la cola, y no me atrevo a deciros lo que hacía con ellos . . .

Durant toute la traversée, la petite vieille n'avait pas cessé de faire part de ses inquiétudes au capitaine qui en était excédé.
Enfin, lorsque le bateau fut à quai il alla lui dire: 'Vous pouvez être tranquille, maintenant, madame, nous avons jeté l'ancre.'
'Ça ne m'étonne pas dut tout,' répondit la petite vieille dame, 'depuis le temps qu'elle pendait du navire!'

Durante tutto il viaggio la vecchia signora aveva continuato a tormentare il capitano.
Arrivati in porto egli le disse: 'Ora signora può smettere di preoccuparsi. Abbiamo buttato l'ancora.'
'Pensavo voleste disfarvene,' disse la vecchietta, 'da giorni la vedevo penzolare lungo la fiancata della nave.'

La viejecita se pasó todo el viaje importunando al capitán con sus preocupaciones.
Por fin, cuando el buque atracó, éste le dijo: —No se lamente más, señora. Ya se ha soltado el ancla.
—¡No me extraña! —contestó la viejecita—. Ha estado colgado de la borda todo el tiempo . . .

'Est-ce que vos avions ont souvent des accidents?' demanda anxieusement la petite vieille dame au pilote.
'Non, Madame. Ça n'arrive qu'une fois!'

Precipitano molto spesso i suoi apparecchi?' chiese ansiosamente al pilota la vecchia signora.
'No, signora! Una volta sola.'

—¿Se estrellan muy a menudo sus aviones? —le preguntó la viejecita al piloto.
—No señora. Una vez tan sólo.

GERMAN

'Shame on you!' said the old lady to the local drunk. 'Every time I see you, you have a bottle in your hand.'
'What do you expect me to do?' said the drunk. 'Keep it in my mouth all day?'

'Sie sollten sich schämen,' sagte die alte Dame zum Betrunkenen, 'immer, wenn ich Sie treffe, haben Sie eine Flasche in der Hand.'
'Soll ich sie etwa den ganzen Tag im Mund haben?' fragte der Betrunkene.

The old lady on her first plane flight was told that pieces of barley sugar would stop her ears popping during the flight. When the plane touched down, the stewardess asked how she was feeling.
'I can't hear you,' said the old lady. 'Not until I can get the barley sugar out of my ears.'

Die Stewardess erklärt der alten Dame, die zum erstenmal fliegt, dass Zuckerbonbons Trommelfellverletzung verhüten, und gab ihr zwei. Als das Flugzeug landete, erkundigte sie sich nach dem Befinden der alten Dame.
'Ich kann Sie nicht verstehen; ich kann diese Bonbons aus meinen Ohren nicht herausbekommen.'

The old lady was worried about crossing the tramlines. An inspector noticed her hesitation and asked if he could help.
'Is it true, young man,' said the old lady, 'that if I put a foot on one of these tramlines I would be electrocuted?'
'No, madam,' said the inspector. 'Not unless you put your other foot on one of the overhead wires.'

Die alte Dame zögerte als sie die Strassenbahnschienen überschreiten wollte. Ein Kontrolleur kam, ihr zu helfen.
'Stimmt es, junger Mann, dass ich einen elekrischen Schock bekommen würde, wenn ich mit dem Fuss die Schienen berühre?'
'Nur, wenn Sie den anderen Fuss an die Drähte da oben halten.'

FRENCH	ITALIAN	SPANISH
'Vous devriez avoir honte!' dit la bonne petite vieille au soûlard du quartier. 'Chaque fois que je vous vois, vous avez une bouteille à la main.' 'Où voulez-vous que je la mette?' répondit le poivrot, 'la garder à la bouche toute la journée?'	'Dovrebbe vergognarsi!' esclamò la vecchia signora rivolgendosi al solito ubriaco. 'Ogne volta che la incontro, ha sempre una bottiglia in mano.' 'Cosa vuole che faccia?' rispose l'ubriaco, 'che me la tenga in bocca tutto il giorno?'	—¡Qué vergüenza! —increpó la viejecita al borracho del pueblo—. Cada vez que le veo lleva la botella en la mano. —¡Y qué quiere que haga! —respondió el borracho—, ¿que la lleve siempre en la boca?
C'était la première fois que la petite vieille dame prenait l'avion. On lui avait dit que si elle prenait des sucres d'orge, cela empêcherait ses oreilles de bourdonner. Après l'atterrissage, l'hôtesse de l'air lui demanda comment elle se sentait. 'J'peux pas vous entendre avec ces sucres d'orge dans les oreilles,' répondit la petite vieille.	Durante il suo primo volo alla vecchia signora fu consigliata una pasticca di zucchero d'orzo per evitare qualsiasi disturbo alle orecchie. All'arrivo la hostess le chiese come si sentisse. 'Parli piú forte,' rispose la vecchietta. 'Non riesco a togliermi queste caramelle dalle orecchie.'	La primera vez que subió a un avión le dijeron a la viejecita que los terrones de azúcar evitan las molestias del oído durante el vuelo. Al tomar tierra, la azafata le preguntó cómo se encontraba. —No oigo nada —respondió la viejecia—. No la oiré hasta que pueda sacarme los terrones de azúcar de las orejas.
La vieille dame hésitait à traverser les rails du tramway. Remarquant son inquiète hésitation, un contrôleur offrit de l'aider. 'Est-il vrai, jeune homme,' demanda-t-elle, 'que si je pose le pied sur un de ces rails, je risque d'être électrocutée?' 'Non, Madame,' répondit le contrôleur, 'non, à moins que vous ne posiez l'autre pied sur le câble électrique qui est au-dessus de votre tête.'	La vecchia signora era preoccupata perché doveva attraversare le rotaie del tram. Un ispettore notò la sua esitazione e le chiese se potesse aiutarla. 'E' vero, giovanotto,' domandò la vecchietta, 'che se metto un piede su una di queste rotaie rimango fulminata?' 'No, signora,' rispose l'ispettore, 'a meno che non metta l'altro piede sui fili lassú.'	La viejecita dudaba antes de cruzar la vía del tranvía. Un inspector observó su vacilación y le preguntó si podía ayudarla. —¿Es cierto, joven —inquirió la viejecita— que si pongo un pie en la vía puedo electrocutarme? —No señora —dijo el inspector—. A menos que ponga usted el otro pie en ese cable de ahí arriba.

THE DEAR OLD LADY

	GERMAN
The Boy Scout saw the old lady laden with shopping bags, struggling on the platform of the bus which was about to move away from the stop. He leapt on the platform, took her shopping bags from her, pulled her inside the bus and sat down. 'It's very good of you,' said the old lady, 'But . . .' 'Please don't mention it,' said the Boy Scout. 'It's my good deed for the day.' 'But,' the old lady went on, 'I was trying to get *off*.'	Der junge Pfadfinder sah, wie sich die alte Dame auf dem Autobustrittbrett mit Einkaufstaschen abmühte. Er sprang hinzu, nahm ihr die Taschen ab und zog sie in den Bus. 'Das war sehr liebenswürdig,' sagte die alte Dame, 'aber . . .' 'Nicht der Rede wert,' sagte der Pfadfinder, 'es ist meine gute Tat für heute.' 'Aber—ich wollte doch aussteigen!'

DEFINITIONS

Money is the only thing that stands between most people and wealth.	Geld ist es, was die meisten Menschen vom Wohlstand trennt.
A pedestrian is a man with a wife, a teenage son and two motor-cars.	Ein Fussgänger ist ein Mann mit einer Frau, einem halbwüchsigen Sohn und zwei Autos.
A bore is someone who talks when you want him to listen.	Ein langweiliger Mensch ist jemand, der spricht, wenn er uns zuhören soll.

FRENCH	ITALIAN	SPANISH
Le boy-scout vit la pauvre petite vieille dame, surchargée de paquets, se débattre sur la plateforme de l'autobus à l'arrêt, alors que ce dernier s'apprêtait à démarrer. D'un bond, il sauta sur la plateforme, débarrassa la petite vieille dame de ses paquets, la tira à l'intérieur et l'assit sur une banquette. 'C'est très aimable à vous, Monsieur,' dit-elle, 'mais...' 'Je vous en prie, Madame,' répondit le boy-scout, 'c'est ma B.A. de la journée.' 'Mais,' reprit la petite vieille dame, 'je voulais *descendre* de l'autobus.'	Il Boy Scout vide la vecchia signora carica di pacchi affannarsi tra la folla, mentre l'autobus stava per ripartire dalla fermata. Saltò sul predellino, s'impo sessò dei pacchi, spinse la vecchietta all'interno dell'autobus e si sedette. 'Lei è molto gentile,' disse la signora, 'ma . . .' 'Non è niente, la prego,' rispose il Boy Scout. 'La mia opera buona per oggi.' 'Ma,' continuò la vecchietta, 'io stavo cercando di *scendere*.'	El Boy Scout vió a una viejecita cargada de cestos que forcejaba en la plataforma del autobús cuando éste se disponía ya a arrancar de la parada. El muchacho saltó a la plataforma, le tomó los cestos, la empujó hacia adentro y se sentó. —Ha sido muy amable —dijo la viejecita—, pero . . —Por favor, no me dé las gracias —respondió el Boy Scout—. Ha sido mi acción buena para el día de hoy. —Pero ... —añadió la viejecita—, es que yo trataba de apearme.
L'argent est le seul obstacle qui sépare de la richesse la plupart de nous.	Il denaro è l'unico ostacolo che si frappone fra la maggioranza della gente e la ricchezza.	El dinero es lo único que separa a mucha gente de la fortuna.
Le piéton est celui qui a une femme, un fils adolescent et deux voitures.	Un pedone è un uomo che ha una moglie, un figlio 'teenager' e due automobili.	Un peatón es un hombre con una esposa, un hijo adolescente y un par de automóviles.
Un raseur est celui qui se met à vous parler au moment où vous voulez qu'il vous écoute.	Noioso è colui che parla quando volete che vi ascolti.	Un pelmazo es alguien que habla cuando quieres que te escuchen.

DEFINITIONS

	GERMAN
A coward is a man who, in emergencies, thinks with his legs.	Ein Feigling ist ein Mann, der in heiklen Situationen mit den Beinen denkt.
A gentleman is someone who raises his hat before he beats his wife.	Ein Gentleman is ein Mann, der den Hut abnimmt, bevor er seine Frau schlägt.
A psychiatrist is a man who goes to a strip club and looks at the audience.	Ein Psychiater ist ein Mann, der sich im Strip-Club die Zuschauer ansieht.
An old maid is a woman who knows all the answers, but never gets asked the questions.	Eine alte Jungfer ist eine Frau, die auf alles eine Antwort hat, aber nie gefragt wird.
A bachelor is a man who doesn't make the same mistake once.	Ein Junggeselle ist ein Mann, der den gleichen Fehler nicht einmal macht.
A bachelor is someone who gets out of bed early in the morning and then goes home.	Ein Junggeselle ist ein Mann, der morgens früh aufsteht und nach Haus geht.
An idiot is anyone who doesn't agree with you.	Ein Idiot ist jeder, der mit uns nicht übereinstimmt.

FRENCH	ITALIAN	SPANISH
Le poltron est celui qui, en cas de danger, réfléchit avec les jambes.	Un codardo è un uomo che, in un'emergenza, pensa con le gambe.	Un cobarde es un hombre que, en caso de emergencia, piensa con las piernas.
Le gentleman est celui qui ôte son chapeau avant de battre sa femme.	Un 'gentleman' è colui che prima di bastonare la moglie si toglie il cappello.	Un caballero es aquel que se quita el sombrero antes de zumbar a su mujer.
Le psychiâtre est celui qui va à un club de striptease pour observer les clients.	Uno psichiatra è un uomo che va a vedere uno spogliarello per osservare gli spettatori.	Un psiquiatra es un hombre que acude a un cabaret y observa a los asistentes.
Une vieille fille est une femme qui connait la réponse à toutes les questions qu'on ne lui a jamais posées.	Una zitella è una donna che sa come rispondere, ma alla quale non vengono mai fatte le domande.	Una vieja criada es la mujer que sabe todas las respuestas, pero a la que jamás preguntan nada.
Le célibataire est celui qui ne commet pas une seule fois la même erreur.	Uno scapolo è un uomo che non ha commesso nemmeno una volta lo stesso errore.	Un soltero es el hombre que no vuelve a cometer el mismo error.
Le célibataire est celui qui se lève tôt, sort du lit, puis rentre chez lui.	Uno scapolo è colui che la mattina si alza dal letto di buon'ora e poi va a casa.	Un soltero es alguien que se levanta muy temprano de la cama y se va a su casa.
Un idiot est celui qui n'est pas d'accord avec vous.	Un idiota è colui che non condivide le tue idee.	Un idiota es todo aquel que no está de acuerdo contigo.

GERMAN

Walking home one night down a dimly-lit street, the man was approached by a villainous-looking and poorly-clad stranger.
'Please, kind sir,' said the stranger, 'can you give me the price of a meal? I have no work, no decent clothes, in fact nothing in the world . . . except this knife and this knuckle-duster.'

Ein Mann wurde auf seinem Heimweg von einem übelaussehendem Kerl angesprochen.
'Bitte, lieber Herr, geben Sie mir Geld für eine Mahlzeit. Ich habe nichts in dieser Welt; keine Arbeit, keine anständigen Kleider . . . nur diesen Schlagring und das Messer.'

The hippy called at his girl friend's pad to take her out on a date.
'Just a minute,' she said: 'I'll just get dirtied up a little.'

Ein Hippy holt sein Mädchen ab.
'Warte,' sagte sie, 'ich bin noch nicht ganz unordentlich.'

The tramp was selling toy balloons in the street. He approached a surly-looking man who said: 'Go away! I don't want your balloons—they stink!'
The tramp drew himself in his tatters up to his full height.
'How dare you!' he said. 'My balloons *don't* stink—it's ME!'

Der Landstreicher verkauft Luftballons auf der Strasse. Er bietet sie einem schlechtgelaunten Mann an.
'Machen Sie dass Sie wegkommen, ich will Ihre lumpigen Ballons nicht haben—einer ist auch schon geplatzt.'
Der Landstreicher streckt sich empört in grosser Würde: 'Nee, das war ich!'

FRENCH	ITALIAN	SPANISH
Un soir qu'il rentrait chez lui en passant par une petite rue mal éclairée, l'homme se vit aborder par un inconnu pauvrement vêtu et à la mine patibulaire. 'S'il vous plaît, mon bon Monsieur,' lui dit l'inconnu, 'donnez-moi de quoi aller manger. Je n'ai ni travail, ni bons vêtements; en fait, je ne possède rien d'autre au monde que . . . ce couteau et ce poing américain.'	Tornando a casa una sera per una strada poco illuminata, un uomo fu accostato da uno sconosciuto mal vestito e dall'aspetto poco rassicurante. 'Sia buono, signore,' disse lo sconosciuto 'mi dia del denaro per comprarmi da mangiare. Non ho né lavoro né abiti decenti . . . difatti non posseggo proprio niente al mondo . . . tranne questo coltello e questo randello.'	Cuando de noche, por una calleja oscura, iba hacia su casa, un hombre vió que se le acercaba un sujeto de mala catadura, pobremente vestido. —Por favor, señorito —le dijo el desconocido—. ¿Podría pagarme el importe de una cena? No tengo trabajo, no tengo un traje decente; en realidad no tengo nada en el mundo . . . excepto este cuchillo y esta cachiporra.
Le hippy alla chercher sa petite amie dans sa piaule pour sortir ensemble ce soir là. 'Un instant,' lui dit-elle, 'donne-moi juste le temps de m'encrasser un peu.'	Un capellone bussò alla porta della sua ragazza e la invito ad uscire. 'Solo un momento, caro,' disse la ragazza, 'aspetta che mi sporco un pochino.'	El hippy le preguntó a su compañera si quería salir con él a dar un paseo. —Espera un momento —dijo la chica—. Tengo que ensuciarme un poco.
Le clochard vendait des ballons de baudruche dans la rue. Il s'approcha d'un passant au visage austère pour lui proposer sa marchandise. 'Allez vous en!' cria l'homme; 'je ne veux pas de vos ballons—ils puent!' Le clochard piqué dans son orgueil, se drapa majestueusement dans ses guenilles et lança, de toute sa hauteur: 'Comment osez-vous me parler de la sorte? Mes ballons ne puent pas, Monsieur! C'est MOI qui pue!'	Un vagabondo che vendeva palloni per la strada si avvicino ad un burbero signore che gli disse: 'Vattene, non so cosa farmene dei tuoi palloni—fanno schifo.' Il vagabondo si drizzò inviperito: 'Non sono i miei palloni che fanno schifo, sono io.'	Un vagabundo vendía globos de juguete por la calle. Se acercó a un hombre con cara de pocos amigos, el cual le dijo: —¡Largo de ahí! No me agradan sus globos. ¡Apestan! El vagabundo se irguió, exhibiendo sus andrajos. —¡Ni hablar, amigo! —exclamó—. Mis globos no apestan. ¡Soy yo!

DOWN AND OUT

GERMAN

The deadbeat approached the mean millionaire.
'Please, mister,' he croaked, 'I haven't eaten anything for three days.'
'Don't be a fool,' said the millionaire. 'Force yourself.'

Der Bettler bittet den Millionär:
'Mister, ich habe seit drei Tagen nichts gegessen.'
'Das ist doch verrückt,' sagte der Millionär, 'zwingen Sie sich dazu.'

'Why don't you take a bath?' shouted the middle-aged man at the two hippies walking along the street.
The younger hippy fell silent. Something was obviously worrying him. After twenty minutes he turned to his friend and said: 'I'm all for new experiences, man, but this one bugs me. What *is* a bath?'

'Ihr solltet wirklich mal ein Bad nehmen,' rief der Mann auf der Strasse den zwei Hippys nach. Das machte den einen Hippy still und nachdenklich. Endlich, nach langer Zeit, sagte er zu seinem Freund:
'Du weisst, wie sehr mich jedes neue Experiment reizt, ich bin auch jetzt ganz scharf—aber was ist ein Bad?'

The hippy enjoyed himself for a while, loafing about and doing nothing. Then he hit the big problem—what could he do on his day off?

Der Hippy vergnügte sich eine ganze Zeit mit Nichtstun und Herumbummeln. Dann stand er plötzlich vor einem grossen Problem: was würde er tun, wenn er einen freien Tag hätte?

FRENCH	ITALIAN	SPANISH
Le tapeur s'approcha du millionnaire avare. 'S'il vous plaît, Monsieur,' dit-il d'une voix enrouée, 'je n'ai rien mangé depuis trois jours.' 'Ne faites pas l'imbécile,' répondit le millionnaire, 'forcez-vous un peu!'	Uno straccione si avvicino a un milionario spilorcio. 'Per carità, signore', implorò, 'sono tre giorni che non mangio.' 'Non fare sciocchezze,' disse il milionario, 'sforzati.'	El pordiosero se acercó al roñoso millonario. —Oiga, señor —le dijo—. Hace tres días que no he comido nada . . . —¡No sea tonto, hombre! —contestó el millonario—. ¡Debe usted esforzarse un poco!
'Allez prendre un bain!' cria le bon bourgeois aux deux hippies qui marchaient à ses côtés dans la rue. Le plus jeune des deux hippies sombra dans un profond silence. Visiblement, quelque chose le tracassait. Après vingt minutes de silence, il se tourna vers son ami et lui dit: 'Je n'ai rien contre les expériences neuves, mais ça, ça me turlupine. Car enfin, qu'est-ce que c'est qu'un bain?'	'Perché non fate un bagno?' urlò un uomo di mezza eta a due hippies che passavano per la strada. Il piú giovane si fece silenzioso e preoccupato. Dopo venti minuti si volse all' amico e disse: 'A me piacciono le esperienze nuove, ma questa proprio non la capisco. Che cos'è un bagno?'	—¿Por qué no os dais un buen baño? —les dijo un caballero de mediana edad a un par de hippies que iban por la calle. El hippy más joven quedó pensativo. Era evidente que algo le preocupaba. Veinte minutos más tarde se volvió hacia su compañero y le dijo: —Mira chico, las cosas nuevas me encantan. Pero ésta me tiene intrigado, ¿qué es un baño?
Le hippy s'amusa quelque temps à trainailler à ne rien faire. Puis un jour, il tomba sur un gros problème: que faire de ses jours de repos?	Per un po' di tempo lo hippy pensò a divertirsi, andando a zonzo e non facendo niente. Ma alla fine si trovò dinnanzi ad un grave problema: che cosa poteva fare nei giorni di festa?	El hippy se pasó un buen rato holgazaneando sin dar golpe. Luego, se enfrascó con el gran problema: ¿qué podría hacer en su día de asueto?

DOWN AND OUT

GERMAN

'A tramp has stolen the cake I left to cool on the window ledge!' cried Mrs Jones. 'Shall I ring for the police?'
'No,' said her husband with a sigh—'for the ambulance.'

'Ein Landstreicher hat den Kuchen gestohlen, der zum Auskühlen auf der Fensterbank stand,' jammerte Mrs Jones, 'ruf' die Polizei an.'
'Nein, die Unfallstelle,' sagte ihr Mann.

The two hippies were stopped at the door of the exclusive restaurant.
'I'm sorry,' said the head waiter, 'but you can't come in here without a tie.' Ten minutes later they were back. One of them was wearing a tie.
'*You* can come in,' said the head waiter, 'but what about him?'
'Him?' said the hippy. 'That's my wife.'

Zwei Hippys wurden gleich am Eingang des eleganten Restaurants abgewiesen.
'Bedauere, hier ist Krawattenzwang,' sagte der Oberkellner. Zehn Minuten später waren die Hippys wieder da. Einer trug eine Krawatte.
'*Sie* können hereinkommen,' sagte der Oberkellner, 'aber der nicht.'
'Der?' sagte der Hippy, 'das ist meine Frau.'

The down-and-out staggered up to the fat, middle-aged matron.
'Lady,' he croaked, 'I haven't eaten for five days.'
'My, my,' said the matron, 'I wish I had your will power.'

Völlig ausgehungert schwankt der Bettler auf die mollige Matrone zu.
'Liebe Dame,' keuchte er, 'ich habe seit fünf Tagen nichts gegessen.'
'Ach lieber Himmel,' rief die Matrone, 'hätte ich doch nur Ihre Willenskraft.'

FRENCH

'Un clochard m'a volé le gâteau que j'ai mis à refroidir sur le rebord de la fenêtre!' gémit Mme Jones. 'Faut-il appeler la police?'
'Non!' répondit son mari en soupirant; 'appelle plutôt l'ambulance!'

ITALIAN

'Un ladro ha rubato la torta che avevo messo a freddare sul davanzale!' grido la signora Jones. 'Devo chiamare la polizia?'
'No,' rispose suo marito sospirando. 'L'ambulanza.'

SPANISH

—¡Un vagabundo me ha robado la tarte que puse a enfriar en el alfeizar de la ventana! —exclamó la señora Jones—. ¿Te parece que avise a la policía?
—No —dijo su marido, ¡avisa a la ambulancia!

Le maître d'hotel d'un restaurant très sélect arrêta les deux hippies au moment où ils allaient franchir la porte.
'Je suis désolé, Messieurs,' dit-il, 'mais vous ne pouvez pas être admis ici sans cravatte.'
Dix minutes plus tard, les deux hippies étaient de retour. L'un d'eux avait une cravate.
'*Vous*, vous pouvez entrer,' lui dit le maître d'hotel, 'mais lui . . .'
'Lui?' demanda le hippie. 'C'est ma femme!'

Duo hippies vennero fermati sull'uscio di un ristorante di gran lusso.
'Sono spiacente,' disse il cameriere, 'ma non possono entrare senza cravatta.'
Dopo dieci minuti ritornarono. Uno dei due aveva la cravatta.
'Lei puo entrare,' disse il cameriere, 'ma il signore no.'
'Il signore?' disse lo hippy. 'Ma quella è mia moglie.'

Los dos hippies se habían visto detenidos a la puerta de un selecto restaurante.
—Lo siento —decía el portero, pero no pueden entrar si no llevan corbata.
A los diez minutos estaban de vuelta. Uno de ellos lucía una corbata.
—Usted puede pasar —dijo esta vez el portero—. Pero y el otro, ¿qué?
—¿El otro? —repuso el hippy—. ¡Si es mi mujer!

Le clodo se dirigea en titubant vers la grosse matronne.
'Madame,' dit-il d'une voix rauque, 'je n'ai pas mangé depuis cinq jours.'
'Eh bien, mon vieux!' répondit-elle, 'si je pouvais avoir ta volonté!'

Uno straccione si avvicinò ad una grassa signora di media eta.
'Signora,' disse, 'sono cinque giorni che non mangio." Perbacco!' esclamò la signora. 'Vorrei avere al sua forza di volonta.'

El vagabundo se acercó a la señora gorda y un tanto madura.
—Señora —murmuró—. ¡Hace cinco días que no como!
—¡Qué bien! —dijo la matrona—. ¡Ya quisiera yo tener tanta voluntad!

THE ARMY

GERMAN

'I can't go in the army,' said the young man at the medical. 'I've got one leg shorter than the other.'
'That's all right,' said the medical officer. 'We'll put you in a mountain warfare unit.'

'Sie können mich nicht einziehen,' sagte der junge Mann zum Militärarzt, 'mein linkes Bein ist kürzer als das rechte.'
'Das ist kein Grund—dann kommen Sie zu den Gebirgsjägern.'

The doctor in charge of the army medical was in a bad mood. When a particularly weedy young man walked in, he took one look and snarled:
'Who sent you—the enemy?'

Der diensthabende Arzt war in übler Laune bei der Reihenuntersuchung. Ein spindeldürrer Jüngling stand vor ihm. Der Arzt gab ihm nur einen Blick und sagte sarkastisch:
'Sie hat bestimmt der Feind geschickt.'

The man had just passed the medical for the army.
'You can't take me,' he protested: 'I wear glasses.'
'That's all right,' said the medical officer. 'We'll put you right at the front so you won't miss anything.'

Der junge Mann wurde nach der Untersuchung diensttauglich befunden.
'Sie können mich nicht einziehen! Ich trage eine Brille!' protestierte er.
'Aber ja,' sagte der Arzt, 'Sie kommen zur Frontlinie, damit Sie nicht daneben schiessen.'

Then there was the soldier who saved the lives of his entire regiment. He shot the cook.

Ein Soldat rettete das ganze Regiment: er erschoss den Koch.

FRENCH	ITALIAN	SPANISH
'J'suis pas bon pour le service,' dit le jeune conscrit au médecin lors de la visite médicale, 'j'ai une jambe plus longue que l'autre.' 'Qu'à cela ne tienne,' répond le médecin de l'armée, 'vous serez versé dans le corps des chasseurs alpins.'	'Non posso arruolarmi,' disse un giovane che stava passando la visita medica. 'Ho una gamba piu corta dell'altra.' 'Non importa,' rispose l'ufficiale medico. 'Ti metteremo nella fanteria da montagna.'	—No puedo ir al servicio militar —le dijo el mozo al oficial médico—. ¡Tengo una pierna más corta que la otra! —¡Muy bien, muy bien! —le respondió el oficial—. ¡Le pondremos en una unidad de montaña!
Le médecin militaire chargé de la visite médicale des conscrits était de très mauvaise humeur. Aussi, lorsqu'un jeune appelé, d'aspect particulièrement rachitique, pénétra dans la salle de visite, il lui jeta un bref regard et aboya: 'Qui c'est qui vous envoie? L'ennemi?'	L'ufficiale medico che stava visitando le nuove reclute era di pessimo umore. Quando un giovane particolarmente macilento entrò nell'ambulatorio, alzò la testa e disse: 'Chi ti ha mandato? Il nemico?'	El doctor encargado del servicio sanitario en el ejército estaba siempre de un humor de perros. Cuando se le presentaba un recluta algo torpe, se le quedaba mirando y le espetaba: —¿Quién le ha enviado? ¿El enemigo?
Il venait juste d'être déclaré 'bon pour le service' par le médecin militaire. 'Vous ne pouvez pas me prendre dans l'armée,' protesta-t-il; 'je porte des lunettes.' 'Ça ira,' répondit le médecin, 'on vous mettra tout à fait aux premières lignes, comme ça vous verrez tout ce qui se passe.'	Una recluta aveva appena passato la visita medica. 'Ma non potete accettarmi,' protestò. 'Porto gli cochiali.' 'Non importa,' rispose l'ufficiale medico. 'Ti metteremo in prima linea cosí non ti sfuggirà nulla.'	Un joven se presentó a la revisión médica. —¡No pueden movilizarme! —protestaba—. ¡Soy miope! —De acuerdo —contestó el oficial médico—. Le mandaremos a primera línea para que no pueda fallar la puntería.
Connaissez-vous l'histoire du soldat qui sauva la vie de tous ses camarades de régiments? Il exécuta le cuisinier.	C'è poi quella del soldato che salvò la vita dell'intero reggimento. Sparò il cuoco.	Hubo una vez un soldado que salvó a toda la compañía. Mató al cocinero.

GERMAN

The officer inspecting the men's rifles looked down the barrel of one particularly rusty-looking weapon.
'Private Parker,' he said, wearily, 'the idea is to shoot the enemy—not spray him with refuse.'

Der Offizier inspizierte die Gewehre. Eins war in einem schlimmen Zustand. Völlig verrosted und der Lauf verstaubt.
'Parker,' sagte der Offizier erschöpft, 'Sie sollen mit diesem Ding den Feind erschiessen, nicht einpudern.'

AT THE DOCTOR'S

The beautiful blonde walked into the doctor's surgery.
'Take your clothes off,' said the doctor.
'But doctor . . .'
'Don't waste my time. I'm busy. Take your clothes off.'
The blonde took off her clothes and the doctor examined her.
'Ridiculous!' he snorted. 'There's not a thing wrong with you.'
'I know that, doctor,' said the blonde: 'I only came in to clean the 'phone.'

Ins Sprechzimmer trat ein bildhübsches blondes Mädchen.
'Ziehen Sie sich aus,' sagte der Arzt.
'Aber Herr Doktor . . .'
'Nun, bitte, ich habe wenig Zeit . . . ziehen Sie sich aus.'
Das Mädchen zog sich aus; der Arzt untersuchte sie.
'Was wollen Sie—Sie sind doch völlig gesund.'
'Ich weiss. Ich will auch nur das Telefon reinigen.'

'Doctor, I've swallowed my pen. What shall I do?'
'Use a pencil.'

'Herr Doktor, ich habe meinen Füller verschluckt —was soll ich machen?'
'Mit dem Bleistift schreiben.'

FRENCH

L'officier qui faisait sa tournée d'inspection des fusils de la brigade regarda longuement à l'intérieur du canon d'un fusil qui lui parut particulièrement rouillé.
'Soldat Parker,' dit-il d'un ton fatigué, 'il s'agit de tirer sur l'ennemi, et non pas de le saupoudrer d'oxyde de fer.'

ITALIAN

Un ufficiale che stava ispezionando i fucili dei soldati ne trovò uno con la canna particolarmente arrugginta.
'Soldato Parker,' osservò esasperato, 'il nemico bisogna ucciderlo, non cospargerlo di polvere.'

SPANISH

El oficial que pasaba revista de armamento se detuvo ante un fusil cuyo cañón aparecía completamente oxidado.
—¡Soldado Parker! —exclamó con enfado—. ¡De lo que se trata es de disparar contra el enemigo, no de rociarle de porquería!

La belle blonde entra dans le cabinet de consultation du médecin.
'Déshabillez-vous,' dit le docteur.
'Mais, docteur . . .'
'Je n'ai pas de temps à perdre. Je suis un homme très occupé. Alors déshabillez-vous!'
La belle blonde se déshabille et le docteur l'examine.
'Ridicule!' s'exclama-t-il. 'Vous n'avez rien du tout!'
'Je le sais bien, docteur,' dit la belle blonde. 'J'étais seulement venue pour nettoyer le téléphone.'

La bella bionda entra nel gabinetto del medico.
'Si spogli,' ordina il dottore.
'Ma dottore . . .'
'Non mi faccia perder tempo. Ho da fare. Si spogli.'
La bionda si denuda e il medico la esamina.
'E' ridicolo,' borbotta. 'Lei non ha un bel niente.'
'Lo so, dottore,' risponde la bionda. 'Io sono soltanto venuta a pulire il telefono.'

La llamativa rubia entró en el consultorio del doctor.
—¡Quítese la ropa —le ordenó éste.
—Pero, doctor . . .
—No me haga perder tiempo. Tengo mucho trabajo. Quítese la ropa.
La rubia se desnudó y el médico procedió a examinarla.
—¡Es absurdo! —dijo el facultativo—. ¡No tiene absolutamente nada!
—Ya lo sabía doctor —respondió entonces la rubia—. Yo sólo vine a limpiar el teléfono.

'Docteur! J'ai avalé mon stylo! Qu'est-ce que je dois faire?'
'Prenez un crayon!'

'Dottore, ho ingoiato una penna. Cosa devo fare?'
'Usi una matita.'

—Doctor, me he tragado la pluma. ¿Qué debo hacer?
—Utilice un lápiz.

GERMAN

The demolition worker was rushed to hospital after collapsing at work.
'I drank a bottle of nitro-glycerine by mistake, doctor,' he croaked. 'I'm afraid to yawn, to cough, even to move.'
'Nonsense!' said the doctor, who suspected the man of malingering. 'There's not a thing to worry about. And just to prove it, I want you to cough, good and hard.'
'I daren't, doctor.'
'You heard what I said. Now cough!'
The man coughed.
'That didn't go *too* well, did it?' said the doctor. 'If you'll just lie down on this little pink cloud, we can try again. I'll hold your harp.'

Der Arbeiter vom Sprengkommando wurde nach einem Kollaps in die Unfallstelle eingeliefert.
'Ich habe aus Versehen eine Flasche Nitroglyzerin getrunken, Herr Doktor. Ich wage nicht, zu husten, zu gähnen oder mich zu rühren,' stöhnte er.
'Unsinn!' sagte der Arzt. Er hielt den Mann für einen Drückeberger. 'Keine Bange! Husten Sie einmal laut und kräftig.'
'Herr Doktor, ich wage es nicht.'
'Husten Sie!'
Der Arbeiter gehorchte.
'Ich glaube, das ging etwas daneben,' sagte der Arzt. 'Das versuchen wir noch einmal. Legen Sie sich auf diese weisse Wolke—ich halte solange Ihre Harfe.'

'My right foot hurts, doctor.'
'Don't worry. It's just old age.'
'But I've had my left foot just as long—why doesn't that hurt?'

'Mein rechter Fuss tut so weh, Herr Doktor.'
'Das sind nur Alterserscheinungen.'
'Aber ich habe den linken doch auch schon so lange.'

FRENCH

L'ouvrier d'un chantier de démolition fut transporté d'urgence à l'hôpital après avoir été pris de faiblesse.

'J'ai bu par erreur une bouteille de nitro-glycérine, docteur,' râla-t-il. 'J'ai la trouille, je n'ose plus bailler, tousser, je n'ose même plus bouger.'

'C'est complètement idiot!' dit le médecin qui soupçonnait l'ouvrier de feindre la maladie. 'Vous n'avez aucune raison de vous inquiéter. Et pour vous le prouver, je vous ordonne de tousser bien fort!'

'Je n'ose pas, docteur!'

'Allons, pas d'enfantillage! Vous avez entendu ce que j'ai dit? Allez, toussez, maintenant!'

L'homme toussa.

'C'était pas très bon, ça!' dit le docteur. 'Ecoutez-moi bien: étendez-vous sur ce petit nuage rose, et essayez encore une fois. Je tiendrai votre auréole pendant que vous toussez.'

ITALIAN

Un operaio di una squadra di demolizione viene portato d'urgenza all'ospedale in seguito as un collasso.

'Dottore, per sbaglio ho bevuto una bottiglia di nitro-glicerina,' spiega con voce fioca. 'Ho paura di sbadigliare, di tossire, persino di muovermi.'

'Sciocchezze!' esclama il medico, che sospetta l'uomo di fingere, 'Non ha la minima ragione di preoccuparsi. E per farle vedere che dico la verità, volgio che dia un bel colpo di tosse.'

'Non oso, dottore.'

'Ha sentito quello che le ho detto, nevvero? Ora tossisca!' E l'uomo tossí.

'Questa volta non è andata *troppo* bene, non le pare?'—constata il medico. 'Se vuol sdraiarsi su questa piccola nuvola rosa, possiamo tentare di nuovo. Il le tengo l'arpa.'

SPANISH

El dinamitero fué llevado al hospital después de haberse desmayado en el trabajo.

—Me he bebido una botella de nitroglicerina por equivocación, doctor —murmuró el infeliz—. Y ahora no me atrevo a bostezar, a toser, ni siquiera a moverme.

—¡Tonterías! —contestó el médico, que sospechaba que aquel hombre se hacía el remolón—. No tiene porqué preocuparse, y para demostrárselo quiero que tosa, que tosa fuerte.

—No me atrevo, doctor.

—Ya oyó lo que le dije. ¡Y ahora, a toser!

El hombre tosió.

—No fué del todo bien, ¿verdad? —repuso el médico—. Si se acuesta usted en esta nubecilla de color de rosa, probaremos otra vez. Yo le sostendré el arpa.

'J'ai mal au pied droit, docteur!'

'Ce n'est rien, ne vous tracassez pas; c'est simplement la vieillesse.'

'Mais enfin, docteur, j'ai mon pied gauche depuis aussi longtemps; pourquoi ne fait-il pas mal lui aussi?'

'Dottore, ho male al piede destro.'

'Non si preoccupi. E' questione d'età.'

'Ma quello sinistro l'ho avuto lo stesso numero di anni. Perchè non mi dà noia?'

—Me duele el pie derecho, doctor.

—¡No se preocupe! Eso es la edad . . .

—Pero es que el izquierdo tiene el mismo tiempo. ¿Por qué no me duele?

AT THE DOCTOR'S

GERMAN

The Australian aborigine went to the doctor, clutching two boomerangs. One was brand-new; the other was old and battered.
'Since I made this new boomerang,' said the aborigine, 'I can't sleep, I can't eat and my nerves are torn to shreds.'
'Come, come,' said the doctor. 'It's a lovely boomerang, but you have obviously put too much effort into making it. It's worn you out.'
'No,' said the aborigine. 'It's the old one that's the trouble. Have you ever tried to throw one of these things away?'

Der Eingeborene kam mit einem alten und einem funkelnagelneuen Bumerang zum Arzt.
'Seitdem ich diesen neuen Bumerang geschnitzt habe, kann ich nicht mehr schlafen, nicht mehr essen und meine Nerven sind völlig aufgerieben,' klagte er.
'Aber warum denn nur? Das ist doch ein wunderbarer Bumerang. Mir scheint, Sie haben zu viel Energie in die Arbeit gesteckt; Sie sind erschöpft,' sagte der Arzt.
'Aber nein, es ist der alte, der mich so fertig macht. Haben Sie schon einmal versucht, einen Bumerang wegzuwerfen?'

ON THE COUCH

The man was shown into the consulting room wearing football boots, a kilt and a top hat. There were daffodils sticking out of his ears and an incense-burner hanging from the end of his nose. In one hand he carried a machine pistol, in the other a watering can.
'Doctor,' he whispered confidentially, 'I've come to see you about this friend of mine.'

Der Mann, der ins Sprechzimmer kam, trug Fussballstiefel, Kilt, Zylinder, in den Ohren Narzissen und an der Nase ein Weihrauchschälchen. In den Händen hatte er eine Maschinenpistole und eine Giesskanne.
'Eine Vertrauenssache, Herr Doktor,' flüsterte er, 'es handelt sich um einen Freund von mir.'

FRENCH	ITALIAN	SPANISH
L'aborigène d'Australie arriva chez le médecin, tenant dans ses mains deux boomerangs. Un était tout neuf, l'autre bien vieux et bien usé. 'Depuis que j'ai fabriqué ce nouveau boomerang,' dit-il, 'je ne dors plus, je ne mange plus et mes nerfs sont en boule.' 'Allons, allons,' dit le médecin, 'voilà un beau boomerang; mais vous avez certainement fait trop d'efforts pour le faire et c'est ça qui a dû vous lessiver complètement.' 'Non, pas du tout,' répondit l'aborigène, 'c'est le vieux boomerang qui est la cause de tout le mal. Avez-vous jamais essayé de vous débarrasser d'un boomerang?'	L'aborigeno australiano si reca dal medico. Ha in mano due boomerang, uno nuovissimo, l'altro vecchio e consumato. 'Da quando mi son fatto questo nuovo boomerang,' spiega l'aborigeno, 'non riesco né a dormire né a mangiare e ho i nervi a pezzi.' 'Su, su, coraggio,' risponde il medico, 'è un boomerang meraviglioso, ma ovviamente frutto di troppi sforzi da parte sua. Il fabbricarlo l'ha esaurita.' 'No,' replica l'aborigeno, 'è quello vecchio che mi preoccupa. Ha mai provato lei a disfarsi di una di queste cose?'	El indígena australiano fué a visitar al doctor llevando dos boomerangs en la mano. Uno de ellos era completamente nuevo. El otro viejo y muy gastado. —Desde que me hice este boomerang nuevo —dijo el indígena— no puedo dormir, no puedo comer y tengo los nervios deshechos. —¡Claro, claro! —respondió el doctor—. Es un bonito boomerang, pero evidentemente, usted ha trabajado demasiado en hacerlo. Se ha esforzado demasiado . . . —¡Nada de eso! —repuso el indígena—. Es el viejo el que me tiene preocupado. ¿Ha intentado usted alguna vez arrojar uno de estos trastos?

L'homme que l'on fit entrer dans le cabinet de consultation portait des chaussures de football, un kilt et un haut-de-forme. Des narcisses lui sortaient des oreilles et il avait un encensoir accroché à son nez. Il tenait d'une main un pistolet-mitrailleur et de l'autre un arrosoir. 'Docteur,' chuchota-t-il sur un ton confidentiel, 'je suis venu vous voir au sujet d'un de mes amis . . .'	Lo fecero entrare nel gabinetto dello psichiatra. Indossava degli scarponi da calcio un gonnellino scozzese ed un cilindro. Dagli orecchi spuntavano dei fiori e dalla punta del naso pendeva un turibolo. In una mano aveva una pistola, nell'altra un' annaffiatoio. 'Dottore,' sussurrò con l'aria da cospiratore, 'sono venuto a sottoporle il caso di un mio amico.'	El hombre entró en el consultorio vestido con botas de fútbol, faldilla escocesa y sombrero de copa. Llevaba un par de narcisos en las orejas, y de su nariz colgaba un incensario. Con una mano sostenía una ametralladora y con la otra, una regadera. —Doctor —musitó confidencialmente—. Vengo a verle a propósito de ese amigo mío . . .

'Tell me,' said the psychiatrist, 'why your family have sent you to me for treatment.'
'It's only because of my passion for currant buns,' said the woman. 'Just because I'm fond of them, they think there's something wrong with me.'
'Ridiculous,' said the psychiatrist. 'Why I'm very fond of currant buns myself.'
'Really?' said the woman. 'Then you must come and visit me. I've got a whole attic full of them.'

'Und warum hat Ihre Familie Sie zu mir geschickt?' fragte der Psychiater.
'Weil ich mit grosser Leidenschaft gern Korinthenbrötchen esse,' sagte die Frau. 'Deshalb glauben sie, dass mit mir etwas nicht in Ordnung ist.'
'Das ist doch Unsinn,' sagte der Psychiater, 'ich esse Korinth enbrötchen auch lei denschaftlich gern.'
'Wirklich? Na, dann müssen Sie mich besuchen—ich habe davon eine ganze Dachkammer voll.'

The delicious blonde was telling her psychiatrist the problem.
'Whenever I have a drink, doctor, I want to make violent love to the first man I see.'
'Don't worry,' said the psychiatrist. 'As soon as I've mixed this cocktail we can sit down and discuss it.'

Die zauberhafte Blondine beschrieb dem Psychiater ihr Problem.
'Herr Doktor, sobald ich etwas getrunken habe, werde ich ganz leidenschaftlich und möchte mit dem nächstbesten Mann ins Bett gehen.'
'Kein Grund zur Aufregung,' sagte der Psychiater, 'darüber werden wir uns einmal in Ruhe unterhalten. Augenblick, ich mixe uns einen Cocktail, dann können wir beginnen.'

FRENCH

'Dites-moi,' demanda le psychiâtre, 'pourquoi votre famille vous a-t-elle envoyée chez moi pour un traitement?'
'C'est à cause de ma passion pour les tartes aux groseilles,' répondit la dame. 'C'est tout simplement parce que j'aime beaucoup ces friandises qu'ils s'imaginent que j'ai quelque chose qui ne tourne pas rond.'
'C'est ridicule!' déclara le psychiâtre. 'Je suis moi-même très friand de tartes aux groseilles!'
'C'est vrai?' demanda la dame. 'Alors, vous devez venir me rendre visite un de ces jours. J'en ai tout un grenier.'

ITALIAN

'Mi dica,' chiede lo psichiatra, 'perché la sua famiglia l'ha mandato in cura da me?'
'Solo perché ho una passione per le brioches con le uvette,' risponde la donna. 'Soltanta perché a me piacciono, loro pensano che ci sia qualcosa di anormale.'
'E' assurdo,' esclama lo psichiatra. 'Cosa vuol dire, quel tipo di brioches piace molto anche a me.'
'Davvero?' risponde la donna. 'Allora deve venire a trovarmi. Ne ho un'intera soffitta piena.'

SPANISH

—Dígame —preguntó el psiquiatra—. ¿Por qué dedea su familia que la someta a tratamiento?
—Sencillamente, porque me pirro por las uvas pasas —dijo la paciente—. Sólo porque me gustan con locura, creen que no debo estar bien del todo.
—Eso es ridículo —repuso el psiquiatra—. !También a mí me gustan con delirio las uvas pasas.
—¿De veras? En este caso debería usted venir a mi casa. Tengo un ático completamente lleno de ellas.

La délicieuse blonde exposait son cas au psychiâtre. 'Voyez-vous, docteur, chaque fois que je prends un verre, j'ai envie de faire passionnément l'amour au premier homme que je rencontre.'
'Ne vous inquiétez pas,' dit le psychiâtre. 'Dès que j'aurai fini de préparer ce cocktail, on pourra s'asseoir et discuter de la chose.'

La deliziosa blonda stava espondo il suo problema allo psichiatra.
'Dottore, ogni volta che bevo, voglio ardentemente fare all'amore con il primo uomo che vedo.'
'Non si preoccupi,' la rassicura la psichiatra. 'Appena ho preparato questo cocktail possiamo sederci e discutere la cosa.'

Una rubia imponente le contaba al psiquiatra su problema.
—En cuanto tomo una copa, me entra un violento deseo de amar al primer hombre que veo.
—No se preocupe —respondió el psiquiatra—. Tan pronto como termine de preparar este cocktail, nos ocuparemos de su caso.

GERMAN

'I just can't help it, doctor,' said the psychiatric patient: 'Every time I go into a shop I can't resist picking things up and putting them in my pocket.'
'Don't worry,' said the psychiatrist. 'I've diagnosed your problem straight away. You're a thief.'

'Es ist merkwürdig, Herr Doktor, wenn ich in ein Geschäft gehe, kann ich einfach nicht widerstehen, dies oder jenes in meine Taschen zu stecken.'
'Die Diagnose ist einfach,' sagte der Psychiater, 'Sie klauen.'

'I have a split personality,' said the patient. 'I keep thinking there are two of me.'
'Could you repeat that, please,' said the psychiatrist. 'And this time don't both speak at once.'

'Bin ich schizophren, Herr Doktor? Ich habe immer das Gefühl, ich bin zwei Personen.'
'Wie bitte? Ich kann Sie sehr schlecht verstehen, wenn Sie beide zur gleichen Zeit sprechen.'

'It's my husband, doctor. For months he's been thinking he's a hen.'
'Good gracious!' said the psychiatrist. 'Why haven't you brought him to me before?'
'I would have done, doctor. But we needed the eggs.'

'Herr Doktor, ich brauche Ihren Rat. Es handelt sich um meinen Mann. Er denkt, er ist eine Henne. Das geht schon so seit Monaten.'
'Ja, aber warum haben Sie ihn da nicht schon längst zu mir gebracht?'
'Wollte ich ja auch. Aber wir brauchten die Eier.'

FRENCH

'Je n'y peux vraiment rien, docteur,' dit le patient à son psychiâtre. 'Chaque fois que j'entre dans un magasin, je ne peux pas résister à l'envie de chiper des choses et de les fourrer dans mes poches.'
'Ne vous tracassez pas,' dit le psychiâtre, 'J'ai diagnostiqué immédiatement votre problème. Vous êtes un voleur!'

ITALIAN

'Dottore, è piú forte di me,' confessa il paziente allo psichiatra.
'Ogni volta che entro in un negozio non resisto: prendo qualcosa e me lo metto in tasca.'
'Non si preoccupi.' risponde lo psichiatra. 'Ho immediatamente diagnosticato il suo problema. Lei è un ladro.'

SPANISH

—No lo puedo evitar, doctor —dijo el paciente al psiquiatra—. Cada vez que entro en una tienda, no puedo resistir la tentación de coger algunas cosas y metérmelas en el bolsillo.
—¡No se apure! —contestó el psiquiatra—. Ya tengo diagnosticado su problema: es usted un ladrón.

'Je souffre d'un dédoublement de la personnalité,' dit le malade. 'Je n'arrête pas de penser que je suis deux personnes à la fois.'
'Pouvez-vous répéter ce que vous venez de dire, s'il vous plaît,' demanda le psychiâtre, 'et tâchez de ne pas parler tous deux en même temps, cette fois.'

'Ho una doppia personalità,' dice il paziente. 'Continuo a pensare che ci siano due di me.'
'Potrebbe ripetere quel che ha detto, per favore,' risponde lo psichiatra. 'E questa volta non parlate tutti e due assieme.'

—Tengo desdoblada mi personalidad —explica el paciente—. Creo que hay dos seres en mi.
—¿Quiere decírmelo otra vez, por favor? —contesta el psiquiatra—. Pero no hablen los dos al mismo tiempo.

'Il s'agit de mon mari, docteur, voilà des mois qu'il se prend pour une poule.'
'Bon Dieu!' répondit le psychiâtre, 'pourquoi ne me l'avez vous pas emmené ici plus tôt?'
'Je sais, j'aurais dû le faire, docteur. Mais on avait tellement besoin des oeufs . . .'

'E' mio marito, dottore, da mesi è convinto di essere una gallina.'
'Diamine!' esclama lo psichiatra. 'E perchè non l'ha portato da me prima?'
'L'avrei fatto, dottore. Ma avevamo bisogno delle uova.'

—Se trata de mi marido, doctor. Desde hace unos meses se cree que es una gallina.
—¡Santo cielo! —dijo el psiquiatra—. ¿Y por qué no me lo ha traído antes?
—Ya lo hubiera hecho, doctor. Pero necesitábamos los huevos.

GERMAN

PSYCHIATRIST: 'Good morning. And what seems to be your trouble?'
PATIENT: 'I keep having the delusion that, when I speak, nobody can hear me. Please do something about it.'
PSYCHIATRIST: 'Good morning. And what seems to be your trouble?'

Psychiater: 'Guten Morgen! Nun, wo drückt der Schuh?'
Patient: 'Helfen Sie mir, Herr Doktor, ich habe diese Wahnvorstellung, dass man mich nicht hört, wenn ich spreche.'
Psychiater: 'Guten Morgen! Nun, wo drückt der Schuh?'

The patient was convinced he had swallowed a horse. Nothing the psychiatrist said would make him change his mind. In desperation the psychiatrist gave him an injection which put him into a deep sleep. When he woke up, the psychiatrist was standing by his bedside, holding by the bridle a beautiful grey mare.
'Nothing more to worry about,' he said. 'We operated on you and took out the horse. Isn't she a beauty?'
'Who are you trying to kid?' snorted the patient. 'The one I swallowed was a jet-black stallion.'

Der Patient blieb dabei, dass er ein Pferd verschlungen hat. Der Psychiater gab ihm deshalb eine Tiefschlafinjektion. Als der Patient wieder aufwachte, stand der Psychiater am Bett mit einer bildschönen grauen Stute.
'Nun ist alles in bester Ordnung! Wir haben Sie operiert und das Pferd herausgenommen. Ein hübsches Tier, nicht wahr?'
'Wollen Sie mich zum besten halten?' empörte sich der Patient.
'Was ich verschluckt hatte, war ein pechschwarzer Hengst, nicht diese Stute!'

FRENCH

Le psychiâtre—'Bonjour! Qu'est-ce qui semble donc vous tracasser?'
Le malade—'Je ne cesse d'être obsédé par l'idée que personne ne m'entend lorsque je parle. Je vous en prie, docteur, faites quelque chose.'
Le psychiâtre—'Bonjour! Qu'est-ce qui semble donc vous tracasser?'

ITALIAN

Lo psichiatra: 'Buon giorno' Cosa c'è che la preoccupa?'
Il paziente: 'Ho la fissazione che quando parlo nessuno mi sente. La prego di fare qualcosa per aiutatmi.'
Lo psichiatra: 'Buon giorno. Cosa c'è che la preoccupa?'

SPANISH

Psiquiatra: —Buenos días. ¿Cuál es su problema?
Paciente: —Tengo la sensación de que cuando hablo nadie me oye. Por favor, dígame que puedo hacer . . .
Psiquiatra: —Buenos días. ¿Cuál es su problema?

Le malade était convaincu d'avoir avalé un cheval. Le psychiâtre avait beau dire, rien ne semblait l'en dissuader. En désespoir de cause, le psychiâtre lui fit une piqûre d'anesthésique qui le plongea dans un profond sommeil. A son réveil, le psychiâtre se tenait à son chevet, tenant par la bride une magnifique jument grise.
'Vous n'avez plus à vous en faire, à présent,' lui dit-il. 'On vous a opéré et on sorti le cheval. Quelle belle bête!'
'Ecoutez!' dit le malade, 'vous vous fichez de moi. Le cheval que j'ai avalé, moi, était un beau mâle tout noir!'

Il paziente era convinto di avere ingoiato un cavallo. Nulla riusciva a fare lo psichiatra per fargli cambiare idea.
Come ultima risorsa, gli fece un'iniezione che lo fece piombare in un sonno profondo. Allorché si svegliò il paziente vide al capezzale lo psichiatra che teneva le redini di una stupenda cavalla grigia.
'Ora non ha piú da preoccuparsi: l'abbiamo operato e asportato la cavalla. E' una bellezza, no?'
'Ma chi sta cercando d'ingannare?' disse il paziente, 'quello che ho ingerito io era uno stallone nero corvino.'

El paciente estaba convencido de haberse tragado un caballo. Nada de cuanto le decía el psiquiatra podía hacerle cambiar de idea. Desesperado, el doctor le puso una inyección que lo dejó profundamente dormido. Cuando despertó, el psiquiatra se hallaba junto a su cama sosteniendo por la brida a un hermoso corcel gris.
—¡Ya no tiene porque preocuparse! —dijo—. Le hemos operado y le hemos extraído el caballo ¿Verdad que es precioso?
—¿A quién trata de engañar? —exclamó el paciente—. El que yo me tragué era un semental negro.

GERMAN

The rising cost of living means that you are now starving on the income you once used to dream about.

Das Leben wird immer teurer. Man kann heute mit dem Einkommen, von dem man gestern geträumt hat, verhungern.

Harry, deep in debt, was sent a bill by a creditor. Written across the top was: 'This bill is one year old.'
Harry sent it back, adding the message: 'Happy Birthday.'

Der völlig verschuldete Harry bekommt eine Rechnung von einem Gläubiger mit der Bemerkung 'diese Rechnung ist ein Jahr alt.' Und Harry schickt sie mit der Bemerkung 'Herzlichen Glückwunsch' zurück.

'Mr Smith,' said the bank manager. 'your account is overdrawn by £200.'
'Let's be reasonable,' said Smith. 'I owe the bank £200. But what was the state of my account three months ago?'
'Three months ago you were £200 in credit.'
'So,' said Smith, 'three months ago you owed *me* £200. And did *I* complain?'

'Ihr Konto ist £200 überzogen,' sagt der Bankdirektor.
'Dann schulde ich also der Bank £200. Sind wir doch vernünftig,' sagte Smith. 'Wie stand mein Konto vor drei Monaten?'
'Da hatten Sie ein Guthaben von £200.'
'Na, sehen Sie, da schuldeten Sie *mir* £200. Und habe *ich* mich beklagt?'

My bank is so big they have a special department for robberies.

Meine Bank ist so gross, dass sie eine Spezialabteilung für Bankräuber reservieren musste.

FRENCH	ITALIAN	SPANISH
La hausse du coût de la vie veut dire que vous crevez maintenant de misère avec un salaire qui n'était pour vous qu'un rêve autrefois.	L'aumento nel costo della vita significa che oggi si fa la fame con lo stipendio che una volta si sognava di avere.	El aumento del coste de la vida significa que te vas a morir de hambre con aquellos ingresos con los que tanto soñabas.
Harry, dans les dettes jusqu'au cou, reçut d'un créancier un rappel de dette. En tête, le créancier avait écrit: 'Cette échéance est vieille d'un an.' Harry la retourna à l'expéditeur avec le mot suivant: 'Bon anniversaire!'	Harry, indebitato fino ai capelli, ricevette un conto da un creditore, con soritto sopra: 'Questo conto ha un anno.' Lo rimandò indietro, aggiungendo: 'Buon compleanno!'	Harry, acosado por las deudas, recibió la factura de un acreedor. En la misma figuraba escrito en la parte superior: 'Esta factura ha cumplido un año.' Harry la devolvió, añadiendo esta frase: 'Feliz cumpleaños.'
'M. Smith,' déclara le directeur de banque, 'votre compte a un découvert de deux mille francs?' 'Soyons raisonnables!' dit Smith. 'Je dois 2.000 F à la banque. Mais qu'y avait-il dans mon compte il y a trois mois?' 'Il y a trois mois, votre compte était créditeur de 2.000 F.' 'Vous voyez!' déclara Smith; 'il y a trois mois, votre banque me devait *à moi* 2.000 F. Je ne m'en étais pas plaint, moi?!'	'Signor Smith,' disse il direttore della banca, 'il suo conto è scoperto per 200 sterline.' 'Ma abbia pazienza!' disse Smith. 'Io devo 200 sterline alla banca. Ma com'era il mio conto tre masi fa?' 'Tre mesi fa aveva 200 sterline a credito.' 'Dunque,' precisò Smith, 'tre mesi fa voi dovevate *a me* 200 sterline. E *io* non ho fatto tante storie.'	—Señor Smith —dijo el gerente del banco—: Su cuenta tiene un saldo en contra de 200 libras. —Seamos razonables—contestó Smith—. Yo le debo al banco 200 libras. Pero, ¿cuál era el estado de cuentas hace tres meses? —Hace tres meses tenía usted 200 libras a su favor. —Eso es —repuso Smith—. Tres meses atrás el banco *me* debía 200 libras. ¿Y acaso me quejé *yo*, entonces?
Ma banque est tellement énorme qu'elle a un service spécial pour les vols.	La mia banca e cosí grande che è provvista di uno speciale reparto rapine.	Mi banco es tan importante, que hasta tiene un departamento para los atracos.

GERMAN

The two bandits were lying in wait with shotguns for the cashier of the big firm who passed the spot at the same time every day on his way to the bank with the takings. But this time he did not appear. The bandits waited for an hour—still no cashier. 'Oh dear,' said one to the other, 'I hope nothing's happened to the poor fellow.'

Mit bereiten Schusswaffen warteten die Banditen auf den Kassierer, der täglich, auf seinem Weg zur Bank, zur gleichen Zeit an der gleichen Stelle mit den Tageseinnahmen vorbeikam.
Aber an diesem Tage kam er nicht. Sie warteten eine Stunde. Kein Kassierer.
'Ich hoffe, dem armen Kerl ist nichts passiert,' sagte einer der Banditen besorgt.

Paddy bought a donkey for £10—all the money he had in the world. But it died. Tearfully he told his friend Mick.
'Don't worry,' said Mick. 'Pretend the donkey is still alive and raffle it. Sell eleven tickets at £1 each and you save your £10.'
'I don't get it,' said Paddy. 'Whoever wins the donkey will be furious—and why £11 to get £10?'
'Easy,' said Mick. 'The winner gets his money back.'

Paddy kaufte für seine letzten £10 einen Esel. Leider starb das Tier sofort. Gebrochen ging Paddy zu seinem Freund.
'Reg' Dich nicht so auf. Tust einfach so, als ob der Esel noch lebt und verlost ihn in einer Tombola. Elf Lose für £1 das Stück—dann hast Du Deine £10 wieder.'
'Das verstehe ich nicht. Elf Lose . . . £1 das Stück . . . damit ich meine £10 wiederbekomme . . . ? Und wer nun den Esel gewinnt, der wird doch wild sein.'
'Verstehst Du das nicht? Wer den Hauptgewinn zieht, bekommt seinen Einsatz zurück.'

FRENCH

Les deux gangsters, armés de fusils de chasse, attendaient le passage du caissier d'une grande firme qui se rendait tous les jours à la même heure à la banque pour y déposer la recette de la journée. Mais cette fois-ci, rien, pas de caissier. Les bandits attendirent encore une heure, toujours rien, pas de caissier!

'Mon Dieu!' soupira un des gangsters, 'j'espère que rien n'est arrivé à ce pauvre homme!'

ITALIAN

Due banditi stavano pronti in agguato, con i fucili spianati, ad aspettare il cassiere di una grande ditta che ogni giorno, alla stessa ora, passava da quel punto per recarsi alla banca con gli introiti della giornata. Ma proprio questa volta non comparve. I banditi attesero per un'ora, poi: 'Mio Dio,' bisbigliò uno di essi, 'speriamo non gli sia capitato nulla di male a quel povero diavolo.'

SPANISH

Los dos bandidos estaban apostados, con sendas pistolas, esperando al cajero de la gran empresa que todos los días pasaba por aquel lugar a la misma hora, camino del banco para ingresar los cobros. Pero en esta ocasión, no aparecía. Transcurrió una hora, y del cajero, nada.

—¡Válgame Dios! —dijo entonces uno de los bandidos—. !Espero que no le haya pasado nada al pobre hombre!

Paddy acheta un âne pour dix mille balles; en fait tout l'argent qu'il possédait; malheureusement, l'animal mourut presqu'aussitôt. Les yeux pleins de larmes, il en fit part à son ami Mick.

'Ne t'inquiète pas,' lui dit Mick. Prétend que l'âne est toujours en vie et organise une tombola. Onze billet à mille balles chacun et tu récupèreras tes dix mille balles. 'J'comprends pas,' dit Paddy. 'Celui qui gagnera l'âne va être furieux; et puis, pourquoi onze mille balles pour en avoir dix?'

'C'est simple,' répondit Mick. 'Le gagnant devra être remboursé.'

Paddy acquistò un somaro per dieci sterline—tutto quello che possedeva—ma l'animale morí. Lacrimando, ne diede notizia all'amico Mick.

'Non stare a preoccuparti,' disse Mick. 'Fa finta che il somaro sia ancora vivo, e indici una lotteria. Vendi undici biglietti a una sterlina l'uno e riavrai le tue dieci sterline.'

'Ma non capisco,' disse Paddy. 'Il vincitore sarà furibondo, e poi perché undici biglietti per riavere dieci sterline?'

'Presto spiegato,' disse Mick. 'Al vincitore restituisci il suo denaro.'

Paddy compró un burro por 10 libras —todo el dinero que tenía—, pero se le murió. Con lágrimas en los ojos fue a contárselo a su amigo Mick.

—No te apures —le consoló Mick—. Haz como si el burro aún estuviese vivo y rífalo. Vende once números de una libra cada uno, y así recuperarás tus diez libras.

—No lo entiendo —dijo Paddy—. El que le toque el burro se pondrá furioso. Y ¿por qué 11 libras para sacar 10?

—¡Muy fácil! —contestó Mick—. Al ganador le devuelves su dinero.

THE ROOT OF ALL EVIL

The mean old man had won a fortune in a sweepstake, but his family didn't like to break the news to him because of his frail condition. Finally they called in his oldest and dearest friend.

'You've known him for fifty years now,' they said. 'And you know how mean he's been all his life. The shock of winning so much money might kill him. So please break it as gently as you can.'

The friend went into the bedroom where the old man lay, tired and ill, on the bed. He asked after his health, talked about the weather, and finally told him, very gently, of his good fortune.

The old man's eyes glistened.

'How's that for a stroke of luck after all these years of scraping and saving?' he said to his friend. 'I'll tell you what—I'll give you half.'

And the friend dropped dead.

GERMAN

Der alte Geizhals hatte ein. Vermögen in der Lotterie gewonnen. Und weil er in einem sehr klapprigen Zustand war, wagte es niemand in seiner Familie, es ihm mitzuteilen. Es wäre ein Schock für den alten Mann, der fatale Folgen haben könnte.

Schliesslich baten sie seinen ältesten und besten Freund, es ihm so sanft wie möglich beizubringen.

Der Freund fand den Alten müde und krank auf dem Bett liegend vor. Langsam und vorsichtig wurde er von seinem grossen Glück unterrichtet.

Die Augen des Alten funkelten.

'Was sagst Du nur dazu? Nach all den vielen Jahren des Sparens and Zusammenhaltens! Weisst Du was—wir teilen uns den Gewinn.'

Aber der Schock, der den alten Freund daraufhin traf, hatte fatale Folgen.

FRENCH

Le vieil avare avait gagné une fortune au sweepstake, mais sa famille ne voulut pas lui annoncer la nouvelle à cause de son état de santé fragile. Finalement, ses proches parents décidèrent de faire appel à son plus vieil et plus cher ami.

'Vous le connaissez depuis cinquante ans, maintenant,' lui dirent-ils, 'et vous savez à quel point il a été avare toute sa vie. Et avoir gagné tout cet argent risque de lui donner un choc fatal. Alors, tâchez s'il vous plaît de lui annoncer la nouvelle aussi doucement que possible.'

L'ami entra dans la chambre où le vieil homme était étendu, usé et malade, sur son lit. Il s'enquit de sa santé, parla avec lui de la pluie et du beau temps et, enfin, lui apprit tout doucement la nouvelle de sa bonne fortune.

L'oeil du vieil homme s'alluma.

'Eh bien! Tu parles d'un coup de pot après toutes ces longues années passées à tirer le diable par la queue!' dit-il à son ami. 'Bon! pour ta peine, j't'en donne la moitié!'

Du coup, l'ami en tomba raide mort.

ITALIAN

Un vecchio avaro aveva vinto un sacco di denaro in una lotteria, ma la sua famiglia non sapeva come fare a dirglielo a causa delle sue precarie condizioni di salute. Finalmente, chiamarono il suo piú vecchio e caro amico.

'Tu che lo conosci da cinquant'anni sai quanto è spilorcio. Lo choc di vincere tanto denaro potrebbe ucciderlo. Perciò diglielo molto cautamente.'

L'amico entro nella stanza, dove il vecchio giaceva a letto stanco ed ammalato. Gli chiese come stava, parlò del tempo, e alla fine gli disse, molto molto cautamente, come era stato fortunato.

Gli occhi del vecchio brillarono.

'Accidenti che fortuna, dopo tutti questi anni di stenti e risparmi,' disse all'amico. 'Sai cosa? Te ne regalo la metà.'

E l'amico stramazzò morto a terra.

SPANISH

El viejo avaro acababa de ganar una fortuna en las apuestas, pero su familia no quería darle esa noticia, puesto que estaba muy delicado. Al fin acudieron a su más viejo y fiel amigo.

—Tu le conoces desde hace cincuenta años —le dijeron—, y ya sabes lo avaro que ha sido toda la vida. La impresión de haber ganado tanto dinero le podría matar. Procura decírselo lo más suavemente posible.

El amigo entró en la habitación donde el viejo se hallaba en la cama, enfermo y cansado. Le preguntó por su salud, hablaron del tiempo y por último, con gran precaución, le informó de su buena estrella.

Al viejo le brillaron los ojos.

—¿Qué te parece este golpe de suerte al cabo de tantos años de estrecheces y de ahorro? —le dijo a su amigo—. Te diré lo que voy a hacer . . . ¡Te regalo la mitad!

Y el amigo se murió de repente.

Smith was angry with his wife.
'I've just had a letter from the bank,' he said. 'You've used up all the money in our account.'
'Impossible,' said Mrs Smith. 'There are still dozens of cheques left in the book.'

Smith war sehr böse mit seiner Frau:
'Ich habe gerade von der Bank einen Brief bekommen; Du hast ja jeden Pfennig, den wir auf dem Konto hatten verbraucht!'
'Unmöglich,' sagte Mrs Smith sorglos, 'da sind ja noch so viele Formulare im Scheckbuch.'

A household budget is a record of what the money should have been spent on.

Ein Haushaltsbudget ist ein klarer Nachweis der schlechten Haushaltsführung.

He had won so much money on the football pools that it went to his head. He started trading in his Rolls-Royce when the ashtrays got full, and then bought a new yacht when the old one got wet.

Das viele Geld, dass der Mann im Fussballtoto gewonnen hat, stieg ihm völlig in den Kopf. Seinen Rolls-Royce tauschte er gegen einen neuen ein, wenn der Aschenbecher voll war; seine Jacht sobald sie nass wurde.

Heard about the idle bandit? He rang up the bank and said, 'This is a hold-up. Send me ten thousand pounds by registered post.'

Der Bankräuber war so faul, dass er den Überfall telefonisch machte: 'Keine Mätzchen, bitte, dies ist ein bewaffneter Überfall! Schikken Sie mir sofort £10000 per Einschreiben!'

FRENCH	ITALIAN	SPANISH
Smith était en colère contre sa femme. 'Je viens de recevoir une lettre de la banque me disant que tu as dépensé tout l'argent qu'on avait,' dit-il. 'C'est pas possible!' répondit Mme Smith, 'le carnet de chèques est encore plein!'	Smith stava bisticciando con la moglie. 'Ho appena ricevuto una lettera dalla banca,' disse. 'Hai finito tutto il denaro nel nostro conto.' 'Impossibile!' rispose la Signora Smith. 'Ci sono ancora dozzine di assegni nel libretto.'	Smith estaba furioso contra su mujer. —Acabo de recibir una carta del banco —dijo—. Y veo que has gastado todo el dinero que teníamos en la cuenta. —Imposible —contestó su mujer—. Todavía quedan muchos cheques en el talonario.
Le budget du ménage, c'est un recueil énumérant tout ce à quoi l'argent du ménage aurait dû être consacré, mais ne l'a pas été.	Un bilancio preventivo amiliare è un elenco di cose che si sarebbero dovute acquistare con il denaro.	El presupuesto familiar es una relación de aquéllo en que debería haberse empleado el dinero.
Il avait gagné tellement d'argent aux pronostics de matches de football que le succès lui monta à la tête. Il commença par donner en reprise sa Rolls-Royce contre une neuve dès que les cendriers en furent pleins; ensuite, il s'acheta un nouveau yacht dès que le premier essuya une averse.	Aveva vinto tanto denaro al Totocalcio che gli diede alla testa. Cominciò con il vendere la sua Rolls-Royce quando i portaceneri erano pieni, e poi acquistò un nuovo yacht quando vide che il vecchio era bagnato.	Ganó tanto dinero en las quinielas, que se le subió a la cabeza. Empezó por venderse el Rolls-Royce en cuanto se le llenaron los ceniceros; luego, se compró un yate nuevo en cuanto el primero se humedeció.
Connaissez vous l'histoire du bandit paresseux? Voilà. Il téléphona à la banque pour dire: 'C'est un hold-up. Envoyez-moi dix mille livres par lettre recommandée.'	La sapete quella del bandito pigro? Telefonò alla banca e disse: 'Questa è una rapina. Mandatemi diecimila sterline a mezzo lettera raccomandata.'	—¿Has oído hablar del bandido perezoso? Asaltó el banco y dijo: 'Es un atraco. Mándenme diez mil libras por correo certificado.'

Joe couldn't sleep. Because of his tossing and turning in bed, his wife couldn't sleep either.
'What on earth's the matter, Joe?' she said.
'I borrowed £50 from Harry Ramsbottom across the street and I can't pay it back.'
Joe's wife was a woman of action. She got out of bed, opened the window and yelled: 'Mrs Ramsbottom!'
After a few minutes a sleepy Mrs Ramsbottom appeared at the window across the street.
'What's the matter?' she yawned.
'My Joe owes your Harry £50. And he can't pay it back,' shouted Joe's wife.
She closed the window and got back into bed.
'Now get to sleep, Joe,' she said. 'Let Harry worry about it.'

GERMAN

Joe wälzte sich restlos im Bett hin und her.
'Was ist los mit Dir?' fragte seine Frau.
'Ich habe mir von unserm Nachbar Ramsbottom £50 geliehen und kann sie nicht zurückzahlen.'
Seine Frau sprang aus dem Bett, lief zum Fenster und rief über die Strasse: 'Mrs Ramsbottom!'
Nach einigen Minuten erschien eine verschlafene Mrs Ramsbottom am Fenster gegenüber:
'Ja, was wollen Sie denn?'
'Mein Joe schuldet Ihrem Harry £50, er kann sie ihm aber nicht zurückgeben.'
Damit schloss sie das Fenster und ging wieder ins Bett.
'So, nun schlaf schön, Joe. Soll Harry Ramsbottom sich jetzt hin und herwälzen.'

A bank is a place where they will lend you money provided you can prove you don't need it.

Eine Bank ist ein Ort wo einem Geld geliehen wird, wenn man nachweisen kann, dass man es nicht braucht.

FRENCH

Joe n'arrivait pas à dormir. Mais à force de se retourner dans son lit, il finit par empêcher sa femme de dormir elle aussi.
'Mais enfin, qu'est-ce qui t'arrive, Joe?' demanda-t-elle.
'J'ai emprunté cinq cent francs à Harry Ramsbottom, notre voisin d'en face, et je ne peux pas les lui rendre.'
L'épouse de Joe était une femme d'action. Elle se leva donc du lit, ouvrit la fenêtre et cria: 'Mme Ramsbottom!'
Après quelques minutes, Mme Ramsbottom, toute ensommeilée, parut à sa fenêtre, de l'autre côté de la rue.
'Qu'est-ce qu'il y a?' demanda-t-elle en baillant.
'Mon Joe doit à ton Harry cinq cent francs et il ne peut pas les lui rendre,' lui cria la femme de Joe.
Puis elle ferma la fenêtre et se remit au lit.
'Maintenant, tu peux dormir, Joe,' lui dit-elle. 'Au tour de Harry de se tracasser!'

Une banque est un lieu où on vous prêtera de l'argent à condition que vous puissiez prouver que vous n'en avez pas besoin.

ITALIAN

Joe non riusciva a dormire. Si voltava e dimenava nel letto, e cosí neppure sua moglie poteva chiudere occhio.
'Ma si può sapere che hai?' gli chiese.
'Ho preso in prestito 50 sterline da Harry Ramsbottom, che vive qua di fronte, e non posso restituirgliele.'
La moglie di Joe era una donna intraprendente. Si alzò dal letto, aprí la finestra e gridò: 'Signora Ramsbottom!'
Dopo pochi minuti la signora Ramsbottom tutta insonnolita comparve alla finestra.
'Che c'è?' sbadigliò.
'Il mio Joe deve 50 sterline al tuo Harry, e non gliele può restituire,' urlò la moglie di Joe.
Chiuse la finestra e tornò a letto.
'E adesso tu dormi, Joe, lascia che sia Harry a preoccuparsene.'

Una banca è un luogo dove ti prestano del denaro a patto che tu possa dare prova che non ne hai bisogno.

SPANISH

Joe no podía dormir. Y como no paraba de revolverse en la cama, su mujer tampoco lograba conciliar el sueño.
—¿Qué diablos te pasa, Joe?—le preguntó al fin.
—Le he pedido prestadas 50 libras a Harry Ramsbottom, el vecino de enfrente, y no puedo devolvérselas.
La esposa de Joe era una mujer de acción. Saltó de la cama, abrió la ventana y gritó: —¡Señora Ramsbottom!
Unos minutos más tarde, aparecía la señora Ramsbottom, soñolienta, en la ventana de enfrente.
—¿Qué sucede? —preguntó.
—Mi Joe le debe a su Harry 50 libras y no se las puede devolver —voceó la mujer de Joe.
Luego, cerró la ventana y se metió otra vez en la cama.
—¡A dormir tranquilo, Joe —dijo—. ¡Que sea Harry el que se preocupe!

Un banco es un lugar donde te prestarán dinero, siempre que puedas demostrar que no lo necesitas.

THE ROOT OF ALL EVIL

Smith and Robinson were business rivals, constantly trying to outdo each other. When Smith painted his shop, Robinson had his shop covered in gold leaf. When Smith bought another shop, Robinson bought a bigger one, right next door to it. When Smith was seen in a night club with a beautiful blonde on his arm, Robinson turned up the next night with two beautiful blondes. When Smith bought a big gleaming car, Robinson bought one too—and hired a chauffeur. In a last desperate attempt, Smith had a telephone installed in his car—only to hear that Robinson had also had a telephone installed. Determined to put a stop to Robinson's antics, Smith rang him up.
'Hello Robinson. This is Smith. I'm speaking from my car.'
'Hello Smith. I'm speaking from *my* car. Could you hang on a second?—there's a call for me on the other line.'

GERMAN

Smith und Robinson sind scharfe Konkurrenten, die sich dauernd zu übertreffen versuchen. Lässt Smith seinen Laden frisch anstreichen, dann lässt Robinson seinen mit Goldfolie übermalen. Kauft Smith ein zweites Geschäft, dann macht Robinson ein grösseres direkt daneben auf. Geht Smith mit einer hübschen Blondine am Arm in einen Nachtclub, erscheint Robinson am nächsten Abend dort mit zwei hübschen Blondinen am Arm. Als Smith sich einen grossen schnittigen Wagen kaufte, hatte Robinson sofort auch einen . . . mit Chauffeur. Der verzweifelte Smith liess sich sofort ein Telefon in seinen Wagen legen und stellte dann fest, dass Robinson bereits ein Telefon in seinem hatte.
Jetzt wurde es Smith zu bunt. Er rief Robinson an: 'Hallo, Robinson, hier ist Smith; ich spreche von meinem Wagen . . .'
'Hallo, Smith, ich spreche auch von meinem Wagen . . . würden Sie bitte einen Augenblick warten? Ich werde am andern Telefon verlangt.'

FRENCH

Smith et Robinson étaient deux commerçants qui se faisaient une concurrence de tous les instants. C'est ainsi que lorsque Smith fit repeindre sa boutique, Robinson fit recouvrir de feuille d'or les murs de son magasin. Lorsque Smith ouvrit un autre magasin, Robinson en acquit un plus grand, immédiatement à côté de Smith. Lorsque celui-ci alla un soir dans un night-club accompagné d'une belle blonde, Robinson alla dans ce même night-club la nuit suivante avec, non pas une, mais deux belles blondes. Lorsque Smith acheta une grosse voiture de luxe, Robinson en acheta une lui aussi et employa un chauffeur. En désespoir de cause, Smith fit installer un téléphone dans sa voiture; mais à peine eut-il fait ça qu'il apprit que Robinson en avait fait de même. Décidé à mettre un terme à la manie d'imitation de Robinson, Smith lui téléphona.

'Allo, Robinson. Smith à l'appareil; je t'appelle de ma voiture.'

'Allo, Smith. Je te réponds de *ma* voiture, moi aussi. Un moment, s'il te plait, on me demande sur l'autre ligne!'

ITALIAN

Smith e Robinson avevano sempre rivaleggiato negli affari. Quando Smith faceva pitturare il suo negozio, Robinson faceva dorare il suo. Quando Smith acquistava un altro negozio, Robinson ne comprava uno piú grande, proprio accanto. Quando Smith si faceva vedere in un night-club a braccetto di una stupenda bionda, Robinson vi compariva la sera dopo con due stupende bionde. Quando Smith comprò una grossa automobile lucente, anche Robinson ne acquistò una, ed ingaggiò un autista. In un ultimo disperato tentativo Smith fece installare un telefono nella sua macchina—e seppe che Robinson aveva fatto lo stesso. Deciso a porre un freno alle stramberie di Robinson, Smith gli telefonò.

'Pronto, Robinson. Parla Smith. Ti telefono dalla mia macchina.'

'Ciao Smith. E io sto parlandoti dalla *mia*. Ti dispiace di rimanere un momento in linea? Sono occupato all'altro telefono.'

SPANISH

Smith y Robinson eran dos competidores que siempre trataban de fastidiarse mutuamente. Cuando Smith pintó su tienda, Robinson decoró la suya con paneles de oro. Cuando Smith compró otro local, Robinson adquirió otro, al lado, mayor todavía. Cuando Smith fue a un club nocturno con una rubia colgada del brazo, Robinson acudió al día siguiente con dos rubias platino. El día que Smith adquirió un coche estupendo, Robinson se agenció otro, con chófer y todo. En un último y desesperado intento, Smith se hizo instalar un teléfono en su automóvil, sólo para enterarse de que Robinson acababa de hacer lo mismo. Decidido a terminar con las extravangias de Robinson, Smith le llamó:

—¡Hola, Robinson! Soy Smith. Te hablo desde mi coche . . .

—¡Hola, Smith! Te hablo también desde mi coche. ¿Puedes colgar un momento? Tengo una llamada por la otra línea.

THE ROOT OF ALL EVIL

	GERMAN
O'Riley was on trial for armed robbery. The jury came out and announced 'Not guilty'. 'Wonderful,' said O'Riley. 'Does that mean I can keep the money?'	O'Riley stand wegen Raubüberfall mit Waffengewalt vor Gericht, aber die Geschworenen sprachen ihn frei. 'Wunderbar!' rief O'Riley erfreut, 'dann kann ich wohl auch das Geld behalten?'

OUT OF THE MOUTHS...

The little boy from the city, on holiday with his uncle in the country farm, was taken to see the sow and her litter. 'Bet you never imagined a pig would be so big, did you?' asked the uncle. 'No,' said the boy, 'but with all those little ones blowing her up, I'm not surprised!'	Der kleine Junge aus der Stadt, der mit seinem Onkel auf dem Lande in einem Bauernhaus Ferien verbringt, sieht zum erstenmal eine Sau mit ihrem Wurf Ferkel. 'Du hast Dir bestimmt ein Schwein nicht so gross vorgestellt,' sagte sein Onkel. 'Nein,' sagte der Junge, 'aber wenn die vielen kleinen Schweinchen es so fest aufblasen, ist das ja kein Wunder.'
Little Jimmy watched his mother shaking flour over a piece of fish before frying it. That evening he saw her sprinkling talcum powder over his little brother at bathtime. 'I'll tell you before you start, mum,' he said, 'you'll need a bigger frying pan.'	Der kleine Jimmy sieht seiner Mutter zu, wie sie Mehl auf einen Fisch siebt und ihn dann bratet. Abends sieht er, wie sie über den kleinen Bruder nach dem Baden Puder streut. 'Mutti, das kann ich Dir jetzt schon sagen—für den brauchst Du bestimmt eine grössere Pfanne.'

FRENCH	ITALIAN	SPANISH
O'Riley comparait devant le tribunal pour vol à main armée. Après avoir délibéré, les jurés le déclarent 'Non coupable.' 'Chouette!' dit alors O'Riley. 'Est-ce que ça veut dire que je peux garder le fric?'	O'Riley fu processato per furto a mano armata. Il giudice lo trovò innocente. 'Meraviglioso!' esclamò O'Riley. 'Vuol dire che posso tenermi tutti i soldi?'	O'Riley era juzgado por un atraco a mano armada. El jurado apareció en la sala y anunció: 'Inocente.' —¡Magnífico! —dijo O'Riley—. ¿Eso significa que puedo quedarme con el dinero?
Le petit garçon qui venait de la ville pour passer ses vacances dans la ferme de son oncle, à la campagne, fut emmené pour voir la truie et sa portée de porcelets. 'J'parie que t'aurais jamais pensé qu'un cochon ça pouvait être si gros, hein?' demanda l'oncle. 'Non,' répondit le gamin, 'mais t'avoueras que c'est pas étonnant avec tous ces petits qui lui soufflent dedans!'	Il ragazzino di città durante una vacanza con lo zio in una fattoria di campagna, viene condotto a vedere la scrofa con i maialini. 'Dí la veritá, non ti immaginavi mica fosse cosí grande un maiale?' chiese lo zio. 'No,' rispose il fanciullo, 'ma con tutti quei piccolini che la stanno gonfiando, la cosa non mi sorprende.'	A un muchacho que vivía en la ciudad le llevó su tío el domingo a la granja para ver a una marrana y a sus cerditos. —Apuesto a que no te figurabas que un cerdo pudiera ser tan granda, ¿verdad? —le preguntó su tío. —No —contestó el muchacho—. Aunque con todos estos pequeños hinchándola como un globo, no me extraña.
Le petit Jimmy regarda sa mère soupoudrer une tranche de poisson avant de la frire. Le soir même, au moment du bain de bébé, il la vit talquer son petit frère. 'J'vais t'dire avant qu'tu commences, maman,' dit-il, 'il te faudra une plus grande poële à frire.'	Il piccolo Jimmy osservò la mamma infarinare un filetto di pesce prima di friggerlo. La sera dello stesso giorno la vide incipriare col borotalco il fratellino dopo il bagno. 'Mamma, sarà meglio che te lo dica prima che tu cominci,' disse Jimmy, 'avrai bisogno di una padella piú grande.'	El pequeño Jimmy observaba como su madre le echaba harina al pescado antes de freírlo. Por la noche vió como a su hermanito, en el baño, le espolvoreaban con polvo de talco. —Antes de que empieces, mamá —exclamó Jimmy—, quiero advertirte que necesitarás una sartén mucho más grande.

OUT OF THE MOUTHS . . .

GERMAN

Sitting next to his mother on the train, little Fred kept tugging her sleeve and whispering urgently in her ear.
'How many times have I told you that it's rude to whisper?' said his mother. 'Speak up, for heaven's sake!'
'All right,' said Fred. 'Why has that man opposite got such a big, red nose?'

Der kleine Fred sitzt neben seiner Mutter in der Eisenbahn. Er möchte ihr etwas ins Ohr flüstern und zupft ungeduldig an ihrem Mantelärmel.
'Wie oft muss ich Dir sagen, dass Flüstern sehr unhöflich ist,' sagte seine Mutter ärgerlich, 'sprich laut, wenn Du etwas zu sagen hast.'
'Na gut: warum hat der Mann uns gegenüber solche dicke rote Nase?'

OUR DUMB FRIENDS

How can you make sure of finding your dog at night?
Feed him garlic all day.

Man kan seinen Hund nachts mit Sicherheit finden, wenn man ihn tagsüber mit Knoblauch füttert.

The gorilla walked into the bar and ordered a pint of bitter. The barman served him and charged him ten shillings.
'Funny thing,' said the barman. 'You're the first gorilla we've had in this bar for years.'
'At ten bob a pint,' said the gorilla, 'I'm not surprised.'

Ein Gorilla kommt in die Bar und bestellt ein grosses Bier.
'Das macht 10 Schilling,' sagte der Barmann. 'Es ist komisch, Sie sind seit Jahren der erste Gorilla, der in diese Bar kommt.'
'Das ist kein Wunder,' sagte der Gorilla, 'wenn Sie 10 Schilling für ein Bier verlangen!'

FRENCH	ITALIAN	SPANISH
Assis auprès de sa maman dans le train, le petit Fred ne cessa pas de lui tirer la manche et de lui chuchoter à voix basse dans l'oreille. 'Combien de fois t'ai-je dit que c'est très mal élevé de chuchoter comme ça?' le gronda sa mère. 'Allez, dis tout haut ce que tu voulais chuchoter!' 'Bon, puisque tu le demandes,' répondit Fred, 'pourquoi que le Monsieur en face de toi il a un gros nez si rouge?'	Seduto accanto a sua madre in treno, il piccolo Fred continuava a tirarle la manica e a sussurrarle insistentemente nell'orecchio. 'Quante volte ti ho detto che è maleducato parlare sotto voce?' gli chiese esasperata la madre. 'Per carità, parla ad alta voce.' 'Va bene,' rispose Fred. 'Perché quell'uomo davanti a noi ha il naso così grande e così rosso?'	Sentado en el tren junto a su madre, el pequeño Fred no paraba de tirarle de la manga y de susurrarle algo al oído. —¿Cuántas veces te he dicho que es de mala educación hablar al oído —le riñó su madre—. ¡Lo que tengas que decir, dilo en voz alta! —Está bien, mamá. ¿Por qué este hombre de enfrente tiene la nariz tan gorda y colorada?
Comment être sûr de retrouver votre chien la nuit? Nourrissez-le d'ail toute la journée.	Come puoi essere certo di ritrovare il tuo cane di notte? Dagli da mangiare dell'aglio di giorno.	—¿Cómo te las arreglas para encontrar al perro por la noche? —Le doy de comer ajos durante todo el día.
Le gorille entra dans le bar et demanda un demi. Le barman le lui servit et lui demanda mille francs. 'Curieux,' dit le barman, 'vous êtes le premier gorille que je vois entrer ici; et pourtant ça fait des années que je travaille dans la boîte!' 'A mille balles du demi,' répliqua le gorille, 'c'est pas étonnant!'	Il gorilla entrò in un bar e ordinò una birra. Il barista lo servì e gli chiese mille lire. 'Che strano,' osservò il barista, 'da tanti anni che sono qui, siete il primo gorilla che mi capita di servire.' 'Non mi sorprende,' fece il gorilla, 'a mille lire al bicchiere!'	El gorila entró en el bar y pidió un doble de cerveza. El camarero se lo sirvió y le cobró diez chelines. —Es curioso —dijo el camarero—. Usted es el primer gorila que ha venido por el bar en muchos años. —A diez chelines el doble —contestó el gorila—, no me extraña.

OUR DUMB FRIENDS

GERMAN

Did you hear the one about the man who crossed a lion with a parrot?
The offspring bit a chunk out of his leg and said, 'Thanks very much.'

Kennen Sie die Geschichte von dem Mann, der einen Löwen mit einem Papagei kreuzte?
Der Sprössling sagte zu ihm: 'Sie gestatten?'—und frass ihn auf.

Then there was the man who crossed a cockerel with a cockerel.
All he got was two very confused cockerels.

Oder die Geschichte von dem Mann, der einen Hahn mit einem Hahn kreuzte?
Was er davon hatte? Zwei bestürzte kleine Hähnchen!

'My dog bit the mother-in-law today, so I've just taken him to the vet.'
'To have him destroyed?
'No—to have his teeth sharpened.'

'Ich nehme meinen Hund zum Tierarzt; er hat heute meine Schwiegermutter gebissen.'
'Wollen Sie ihn töten lassen?'
'Nein—seine Zähne müssen schärfer gemacht werden.'

A flea rushed into the bar just before closing time, ordered five double scotches, drank them straight down, rushed into the street, jumped high in the air and fell flat on his face.
'Darn it,' he muttered as he picked himself up. 'Someone has moved my dog.'

Ein Floh sprang eilig kurz vor Polizeistunde in die Bar, bestellte fünf doppelte Whiskys, trank sie, hüpfte wieder raus, sprang hoch in die Luft ... und landete flach auf seinem Gesicht.
'Verdammt,' fluchte er, 'jemand hat meinen Hund weggenommen!'

FRENCH	ITALIAN	SPANISH
Savez-vous ce qui est arrivé au bonhomme qui fit un croisement entre un lion et un perroquet? Le petit lui bouffa un gros morceau de la jambe et lui dit: 'Merci beaucoup!'	Avete sentito quella dell'uomo che decise di accoppiare un leone con un pappagallo? Ne nacque uno strano animale, che gli morsicò un pezzo di gamba e disse: 'Grazie mille.'	¿Oiste hablar de aquel hombre que cruzó una leona y un loro? Pues el bicho que salió, le pegó un mordisco en la pierna y le dijo 'Muchas gracias.'
Et puis il y a l'histoire de celui qui essaya un croisement entre deux coqs. Résultat: deux coqs très névrosés.	E poi c'era l'uomo che accoppiò due galletti. Il risultato: due galletti molto, molto confusi.	También hubo un hombre que cruzó un gallo con otro gallo. Lo único que obtuvo fueron dos gallos desorientados.
'Mon chien a mordu aujourd'hui ma belle-mère; aussi, je l'ai emmené chez le vétérinaire.' 'Pour le faire piquer?' 'Non! pour lui faire aiguiser les canines.'	'Oggi il mio cane ha morso mia suocera, e cosí l'ho portato subito dal veterinario.' 'Per farlo uccidere?' 'No, per fargli affilare i denti.'	—Hoy mi perro ha mordido a mi suegra, y lo he llevado al veterinario. —¿Para que lo mate? —No. Para que le afile los dientes.
Une puce se précipita dans le bar juste avant la fermeture, commanda cinq grands Scotch, les avala d'une traite, fonça ensuite vers la rue, sauta en l'air et s'écrasa la gueule sur le trottoir. 'Merde!' murmura-t-elle en se relevant péniblement. 'Quelqu'un a bougé le chien!'	Una pulce entrò di corsa nel bar, proprio prima che chiudesse, ordinò cinque doppi whiskies, li bevve uno dopo l'altro, corse per la strada, spiccò un salto e cadde pesantemente per terra. 'Accidenti,' mormorò rialzandosi, 'qualcuno ha spostato il mio cane.'	Una pulga entró precipitadamente en un bar momentos antes de que cerrasen, pidió cinco whiskies dobles, se los bebió, salió de nuevo a la calle, brincó en el aire y cayó de bruces al suelo. —¡Maldita sea! —exclamó al levantarse—. ¡Alguien ha cambiado de sitio mi perro!

GERMAN

O'Toole had a donkey which was eating him into the poorhouse. He decided to put it on a diet and see how little it could live on. Every day he gave it less and less food, until finally he gave it nothing at all.
Then the donkey died.
'What do you think of that?' said O'Toole. 'He ups and dies just as he's getting used to not eating!'

O'Toole hatte einen Esel, der ihm die Haare vom Kopf frass.
Er entschloss sich, ihn auf Diät zu setzen, und ihm jeden Tag etwas weniger Futter zu geben. Es würde sich ja herausstellen, mit wie wenig er auskommen kann.
Immer weniger gab er ihm —und eines Tages nichts mehr.
Und da starb der Esel.
'So ein Pech,' sagte O'Toole, 'er hat sich so schön ans Nichtessen gewöhnt und da schrammt er ab.'

The big game hunter heard a terrible scream from his friend ahead of him in the jungle.
'What's the matter?' he shouted.
'A lion has bitten off my foot,' came the agonised reply.
'Which one?'
'How should I know? All these lions look alike to me.'

Zwei Freunde sind im Urwald auf der Löwenjagd. Plötzlich schreit der eine laut auf.
'Was ist denn um Gottes-willen los?' fragte sein Freund.
'Ein Löwe hat mir meinen Fuss abgebissen . . . mein Fuss, mein Fuss!'
'Welcher?'
'Welcher Löwe???? Wie soll ich das wissen, die sehen doch alle gleich aus.

How do hedgehogs make love? Very, very carefully.

Wie machen Igel ihre Kinder?
Sehr, sehr vorsichtig.

FRENCH	ITALIAN	SPANISH
O'Toole avait un âne qui lui coûtait tellement cher à entretenir que le pouvre O'Toole se voyait déjà sur le chemin de la ruine. Finalement, il décida de rationner l'âne et de le mettre au régime afin de déterminer la plus petite ration qui lui serait nécessaire pour vivre. Chaque jour, donc, il lui donna un peu moins à manger; jusqu'au jour où à force de diminuer sa ration, il ne lui donna plus rien du tout. L'âne finit par en mourir. 'Ça par exemple!' dit O'Toole, 'il a choisi de mourir juste au moment où il commençait à s'habituer à ne plus manger!'	O'Toole aveva un asino che gli mangiava una costola al giorno. Decise di metterlo a dieta per vedere con quanto poco avrebbe potuto campare. Gli diminuí ogni giorno i pasti, finché, un bel giorno, non gli diede nulla. E l'asino morí. 'Bel tipo, eh?' fece O'Toole, 'decide di morire proprio ora che si è abituato a non mangiare nulla.'	O'Toole tenía un asno que le costaba un ojo de la cara de mantener. Por eso decidió ponerlo a régimen y ver hasta qué punto podía rebajarle la dieta. Día tras día iba dándole menos comida, hasta que al fin no le dió nada en absoluto. Entonces el asno se murió. —¿Qué te parece? —decía O'Toole—. ¡Se da por vencido y se muere cuando ya empezaba a acostumbrarse a no comer!
Le chasseur de fauves entendit un hurlement terrible de la part de son ami qui le précédait dans la jungle. 'Qu'est ce qu'il y a?' lui cria-t-il. 'Un lion vient de me bouffer le pied,' répondit l'autre d'une voix agonisante. 'Lequel?' 'Comment veux-tu que je sache? Pour moi, tous les lions se ressemblent!'	Il cacciatore di leoni udí un urlo agghiacciante proveniente dal mezzo della giungla dove si trovava il suo compagno. 'Che cosa succede?' gridò. 'Un leone mi ha mangiato un piede.' 'Quale?' 'E che ne so io, tutti questi leoni si rassomigliano.'	El gran cazador oyó un terrible grito que lanzó su amigo, que le precedía en la selva. —¿Qué passa? —preguntó. —Un león me ha mordido en el pie —fue la angustiada respuesta. —¿Cuál? —¡Yo que sé! ¡Todos los leones me parecen iguales!
Comment le hérisson fait-il l'amour? En faisant très, très attention!	Come fanno all'amore i porcospini? Molto, molto cautamente.	¿Cómo se hacen el amor los erizos? Con mucho, muchísimo cuidado.

GERMAN

Carrots must be good for your eyes—have you ever seen a rabbit with glasses?

Karotten sind wirklich gut für die Augen—oder hast Du schon ein Kaninchen mit Brille gesehen?

'Excuse me mentioning this,' said the elephant to the mouse, 'but you're very small.'
'I know,' said the mouse. 'I've not been very well.'

'Sei mir nicht böse, wenn ich es erwähne,' sagt der Elefant zur Maus, 'aber Du bist sehr klein.'
'Ich weiss,' sagt die Maus, 'es ging mir in letzter Zeit nicht sehr gut.'

The zoo elephant died, and its keeper was sitting by the corpse weeping bitterly.
'There, there, now,' said an old lady who was passing. 'Try to be brave. I know how fond you must be of the dear animal after taking care of it for all these years.'
'Fond, nothing,' snapped the keeper. 'I've got to bury the damn thing!'

Der Wärter sass neben dem toten Elefanten im Zoo und weinte bitterlich. Eine alte Dame kam zu ihm und wollte ihn trösten.
'Sie haben das liebe Tier jahrelang betreut; ich kann mir vorstellen, wie Sie sich grämen.'
'Grämen? Keine Spur! Ich weine, weil ich dieses verdammte Ding begraben muss!'

Heard about the millionaire flea who bought a pack of hounds?

Der Floh des Millionärs konnte es sich leisten, eine Meute zu kaufen.

FRENCH	ITALIAN	SPANISH
Les carottes sont bonnes pour la vue. Avez-vous jamais vu un lapin avec des lunettes?	Le carote devono fare bene alla vista—avete mai visto un coniglio con gli occhiali?	Las zanahorias deben ser buenas para los ojos. ¿Has visto alguna vez a un conejo con gafas?
'Excusez-moi d'avoir à le dire, mais vous êtes minuscule!' dit l'éléphant à la souris. 'Je sais,' répliqua celle-ci, 'j'ai été souffrante ces derniers temps.'	'Non se l'abbia a male,' disse l'elefante al topo, 'ma lei è veramente molto piccolo.' 'Lo so,' rispose il topo: 'Sono stato poco bene.'	—Perdóname que te lo diga —le habló el elefante al ratón—. Pero eres muy pequeño. —Ya lo sé —respondió el ratón—. ¡Es que no he estado muy bien últimamente!
Au zoo, l'éléphant venait de mourir et son gardien s'était assis sur le corps de l'énorme bête, pleurant de chagrin. 'Allons, allons,' dit une vieille dame qui passait par là; 'du courage, mon brave homme. Je sais combien vous l'aimiez votre cher éléphant après tant d'années!' 'Aimer, mon cul!' éclata le gardien. 'Vous n'savez pas c'que c'est d'avoir à enterrer cette sale bête!'	L'elefante del giardino zoologico era morto, ed il guardiano stava seduto accanto al cadavere singhiozzando disperatamente. 'Non se la prenda tanto a cuore,' disse una vecchietta che passava di lí, 'si faccia coraggio. Capisco quanto deve aver amato la povera bestia dopo averla curata per tanti anni.' 'Amato un corno,' sbofonchiò il guardiano, 'mi tocca di seppellirlo, questo accidente!'	El elefante del zoológico acababa de morir, y su cuidador lloraba amargamento junto a su cuerpo. —¡Vamos, vamos! —dijo una señora que pasaba por allí—. ¡Tenga valor, hombre! Ya me imagino que debía querer mucho al pobre animal, después de cuidarlo tantos años. —¡Nada de eso, señora! —exclamó el cuidador—. ¡Lo peor es que no tengo más remedio que enterrarlo!
Connaissez-vous l'histoire de la puce qui, devenue millionnaire, s'est acheté toute une meute de chiens?	Avete sentito quella della pulce milionaria che si è comprata una muta di cani?	—¿Has oído hablar de aquella pulga millonaria que se compró una jauría de perros?

GERMAN

The vicar was taking tea with the old lady and was very impressed with her talking parrot.
'But tell me, dear lady,' he said, 'why does the parrot have a piece of string tied to each leg?'
'If you pull the string on the right leg,' said the old lady, 'he sings Onward Christian Soldiers. And if you pull the other string he sings Nearer My God To Thee.'
'What happens,' said the vicar, 'if you pull both strings at once?'
'I fall off my perch, you silly old fool,' said the parrot.

Der Pfarrer besuchte die alte Dame zum Tee und war sehr beeindruckt von ihrem Papagei.
'Aber sagen Sie mir bitte, liebe gnädige Frau, warum hat er an jedem Bein eine Schnur?'
'Zum Singen,' erklärt die alte Dame. 'Wenn ich die rechte Schnur ziehe, dann singt er "Wir danken alle Gott" und wenn ich die linke ziehe, singt er "Näher, mein Gott, zu dir".'
'Und was macht er, wenn Sie beide ziehen?' wollte der Pfarrer wissen.
'Dann falle ich von der Stange, Sie blöder Kerl,' sagte der Papagei.

Two boy centipedes were standing on the corner when a girl centipede passed.
'Look at that!' said one boy centipede admiringly. 'That's what I call a good pair of legs . . . pair of legs . . . pair of legs . . .'

Zwei junge Tausendfüssler standen an der Ecke, als eine junge Tausendfüsslerin vorbeiging.
'Na sieh' mal . . .' sagte der eine Tausendfüssler, 'das nenne ich ein paar schöne Beine . . . ein paar schöne Beine . . . ein paar schöne Beine . . .'

FRENCH	ITALIAN	SPANISH
Le curé prenait le thé avec la vieille dame et il était très impressionné par les prouesses vocales de son perroquet. 'Dites-moi, chère Madame,' demanda-t-il, 'mais pourquoi votre perroquet a-t-il un morceau de ficelle attaché à chaque patte?' 'Si vous tirez la ficelle de la patte droite,' répondit la vieille dame, 'il se met à chanter "En avant, soldat du Christ!" Si vous tirez la ficelle de la patte gauche, il entonne "Plus près de toi Mon Dieu!" ' 'C'est remarquable!' dit le curé; 'mais qu'arrive-t-il si on tire les deux ficelles à la fois?' 'J'me casse la gueule, eh vieux croûton!' répliqua le perroquet.	Il parroco stava prendendo il tè con la vecchia signora, e ne ammirava il pappagallo parlante. 'Ma mi dica, cara signora, perché il pappagallo ha due spaghi legati alle zampe?' Se si tira lo spago attaccato alla zampa destra, disse la signora, canta un inno religioso, Se quello a sinistra, una marcia militare.' 'Che cosa succede,' chiese il parroco, se si tirano tutti e due gli spaghi insienme?' 'Pezzo di cretino,' urlò l'uccello, 'casco dal posatoio.'	El vicario se hallaba tomando el té con la anciana señora, y estaba admirado de su loro parlanchín. —Dígame, señora —preguntó—. ¿Por qué este loro lleva un trocito de cordel en cada pata? —Si tira usted del cordel de la pata derecha —explico la dama—, canta el 'Adelante soldados de Cristo.' Y si tira del otro cordel, entona el 'Más cerca de Ti, mi Dios.' —¿Y qué ocurre —dijo el vicario— si se tira de los dos cordeles a un tiempo? —¡Que me caigo de la percha, bobo! —contestó el loro.
Deux jeunes mille-pattes mâles discutaient au coin d'une rue lorsque vint à passer une jeune femelle mille-pattes. 'Vise-moi ça!' siffla admirativement un des jeunes mille-pattes. 'Voilà c'que j'appelle une belle paire de jambes . . . paire de jambes . . . paire de jambes . . .!'	Due giovani millepiedi stavano ad un angolo della strada, quando ecco avanzarsi una millepiedi femmina. 'Guarda un pó',' disse uno dei millepiedi maschi, quello sí che è un bel paio di gambe, paio di gambe . . . paio di gambe . . .	Dos ciempiés machos se hallaban en una esquina, cuando pasó por allí un ciempiés hembra. —Mira eso —exclamó con admiración uno de ellos—. ¡A eso le llamo yo un buen par de piernas . . . par de piernas . . . par de piernas . . .!

GERMAN

'A dozen mouse-traps, please,' asked the man.
'Certainly, sir,' said the ironmonger. 'Do you want to take them with you?'
'No,' said the man sarcastically, 'I'll send the mice over here.'

'Ein Dutzend Mausefallen,' verlangte der Mann von dem Verkäufer.
'Wollen Sie sie mitnehmen?' fragte dieser wohltrainiert.
'Nein,' sagte der Mann sarkastisch, 'ich schicke die Mäuse hierher.'

'Give us a kiss,' said the worm.
'Don't be silly,' said the second worm: 'I'm your other end.'

'Küsschen, Küsschen!' sagte der Wurm zum andern.
'Sei bitte nicht so albern! Wir gehören doch zusammen.'

The theatrical agent had had a tiring day.
'Look,' he said to the last applicant, 'don't waste my time unless you've got something really special.'
'Just watch this,' said the applicant.
He flapped his arms and flew around the room, alighting on the agent's desk where he laid an egg.
'O.K., so you can imitate birds,' said the agent. 'What else do you do?'

Der Agent hatte einen anstrengenden Tag hinter sich, deshalb sagte er zum letzten Bewerber:
'Vergeuden Sie nicht meine Zeit, wenn Sie nichts besonderes zu bieten haben.'
Der junge Mann war seiner Sache sicher. Er machte Flügelschläge mit seinen Armen, flatterte durch den Raum, landete auf dem Schreibtisch und legte ein Ei.
'O.K., Sie könnern Vögel imitieren—ist das alles?'

FRENCH	ITALIAN	SPANISH
'Une douzaine de souricières, s'il vous plaît,' demanda le client. 'Tout de suite Monsieur,' répondit le quincailler. 'C'est pour emporter avec vous?' 'Non!' répliqua avec sarcasme le client, 'je vous enverrai les souris ici.'	'Una dozzina di trappole per topi, per favore,' chiese l'uomo. 'Certamente, signore,' rispose il negoziante, 'e le porta via con sé?' 'No,' rispose l'uomo con sarcasmo, 'le manderò i topi qui.'	—Una docena de ratoneras, por favor —pidió un hombre. —Sí, señor —le dijo el ferretero—. ¿Quiere llevárselas usted mismo? —No —respondió el hombre sarcásticamente—. Le mandaré aquí los ratones.
'Donne-moi un baiser . . .' susurra le ver de terre. 'Fais pas le con,' répondit l'autre, 'j'suis ton autre extrémité!'	'Baciami,' disse il verme. 'Non fare lo scemo,' rispose l'altro verme, 'non vedi che sono la tua coda?'	—¡Dame un beso! —dijo el gusano. —¡No seas bobo —le respondió el otro—. Yo soy tu otro extremo.
L'imprésario avait eu une journée fatigante. 'Ecoutez,' dit-il au dernier artiste qui avait pris rendez-vous avec lui, 'ne me faites pas perdre mon temps si vous n'avez rien de vraiment sensationnel à me proposer!' 'Regardez simplement ça,' dit l'artiste en quête de travail. Et, battant des bras, il vola tout autour de la pièce, puis se posa sur le bureau de l'imprésario et y pondit un oeuf.' Bon, vous pouvez imiter les oiseaux,' dit l'imprésario. 'Qu'est-ce que vous savez faire d'autre?'	L'impresario aveva avuto una giornata pesante. 'Senta,' disse all'ultimo candidato, 'non sprechi il mio tempo a meno che non mi possa offrire qualche cosa di veramente straordinario.' 'Guardi!' disse il candidato. Sbatté le braccia e svolazzò attorno alla stanza, si fermò sul tavolo dell'impresario e vi posò un uovo. 'Va bene, va bene,' disse l'impresario, 'sa imitare gli uccelli, ma che cosa altro sa fare?'	El agente teatral había tenido un día agotador. —Mire usted —le dijo al último solicitante—. No me haga perder tiempo si no tiene nada realmente especial que ofrecerme. —Fíjese en eso —le contestó el aspirante. Y batiendo los brazos empezó a volar por la habitación, posándose luego en la mesa del agente, donde puso un huevo. —Muy bien. Así que imita a los pájaros —dijo el agente—. ¿Y qué más sabe hacer?

GERMAN

The horse ran last in the big race, and the owner was haranguing the jockey.
'Surely, man,' bellowed the owner, 'you could have moved faster than that!'
'Easily,' said the jockey, 'but I had to stay with the horse.'

Der Rennstallbesitzer nahm sich seinen Jockey vor, weil das Pferd beim grossen Rennen als letztes durchs Ziel kam.
'Zum Donnerwetter! Sie hätten doch bestimmt schneller sein können!'
'Ohne weiteres. Aber ich musste ja bei dem Pferd bleiben.'

The big man walked into the bar and ordered six pints of beer and six whiskies. He drank the beer straight down, poured the whiskies into his top pocket, ordered the same again and did the same thing: drank the beer and poured the whiskies into his top pocket.
'Pardon me,' said the barman, 'but why do you drink the beer and pour the whisky into your top pocket?'
'Mind your own business,' said the big man, 'or I'll kick your teeth in.'
A little mouse popped its head out of the big man's pocket.
'And that goes for your cat as well,' it hiccoughed.

Ein Riesenkerl kommt in die Bar, bestellt sechs grosse Biere und sechs Whiskys. Die Biere trinkt er sofort, die Whiskys schüttet er in seine Westentasche. Er bestellt noch einmal dasselbe; trinkt die Biere, schüttet die Whiskys in die Westentasche.
Der Barmann wurde neugierig.
'Entschuldigen Sie, aber warum machen Sie das . . . ?'
'Kümmern Sie sich um Ihren Kram, sonst schlage ich Ihnen die Zähne ein!'
Bei diesen Worten steckte eine völlig betrunkenen kleine Maus ihren Kopf aus der Westentasche und sagte zum Barmann:
'Das können Sie auch Ihrer Katze bestellen.'

FRENCH	ITALIAN	SPANISH
Le cheval était arrivé dernier au Grand Prix et le propriétaire, pas content du tout, s'en prit au jockey. 'Enfin, tout de même,' hurla-t-il, 'vous auriez pu aller plus vite que ça!' 'Facilement,' répondit le jockey; 'mais je devais quand même rester avec le cheval.'	Il cavallo era arrivato ultimo nella grande corsa, e il proprietario stava sgridando il fantino. 'Ma dico, non ti saresti potuto muovere un po' piú velocemente?' 'Certamente,' rispose il fantino, 'ma dovevo rimanere con i cavalli.'	El caballo se había quedado el último en la gran carrera, y el propietario discutía con el jockey. —¡Estoy seguro de que hubieras podido correr mucho más! —¡Ya lo creo! —respondió el jockey—. Pero tenía que quedarme con los caballos, ¿no?
Le malabar se dirigea vers le comptoir, commanda six demis de bière et six whiskies. Il but d'une seule traite les six verres de bière et versa le whisky dans la pochette de son veston. Puis il commanda encore six autres bières et six autres whiskies et refit exactement la même chose. 'Excusez-moi, Monsieur,' dit le barman, 'mais pouvez vous me dire pourquoi vous buvez la bière et verser le whisky dans votre pochette de veston?' 'Mêlez-vous de vos affaires,' dit le malabar, 'sinon, j'vous casse la figure.' Une petite souris sortit alors la tête de la pochette du veston du malabar et dit d'une petite voix avinée: 'Et si ton chat n'est pas content, on f'ra pareil avec lui!'	Un omaccione entrò nel bar e ordinò sei litri di birra e sei whiskies. Tracannò la birra, versò il whisky nel taschino della giacca, ripetè l'ordinazione e fece la stessa cosa: bevve la birra e versò il whisky nel taschino. 'Mi scusi,' disse il barista, 'ma perché beve la birra e versa il whisky nel taschino?' 'Bada ai fatti tuoi,' rispose l'omaccione, 'o ti arriva un malrovescio.' Un topolino si affacciò al taschino dell'omaccione. 'E questo vale per il suo gatto,' affermò con voce da ubriaco.	El hombrachón entró en el bar y pidió seis dobles de cerveza y seis whiskies. Se bebió la cerveza de un tirón y vertió los whiskies en el bolsillo superior de la chaqueta. Otra vez pidió lo mismo y repitió indéntica operación: se bebió la cerveza y vertió el whisky en el bolsillo. —Perdone —dijo el barman—, pero ¿por qué se bebe la cerveza y se echa el whisky en el bolsillo? —¡No se meta con lo que no le importa —contestó el hombrachón—, o le partiré las muelas de un puñetazo. Un ratoncito asomó entonces la cabeza por el borde del bolsillo: —¡Eso mismo vale también para su gato —masculló.

GERMAN

Heard about the poor firefly who died trying to make love to a cigarette end?

Kennen Sie die Geschichte von dem armen Leuchtkäfer, der sich leidenschaftlich auf eine brennende Zigarette stürzte?

The furrier and the accountant were on safari in the jungle, getting more and more lost and more and more frightened. There was a terrifying roar and a gigantic beast leapt on the furrier's back. 'For heaven's sake!' he screamed. 'What's that thing on my back?'
'Don't ask me,' said his companion. '*You're* the furrier.'

Der Kürschner war mit seinem Rechnungsführer auf Safari.
Sie verirrten sich im Dschungel immer mehr und wurden immer ängstlicher.
Plötzlich sprang ein schreckliches Biest mit furchtbarem Gebrüll dem Kürschner auf den Rücken.
'Hilfe! Um Gottes Willen—was habe ich da auf meinem Rücken?'
'Wie soll ich das wissen,' sagte sein Begleiter, 'Du bist der Pelzfachmann!'

The bats in their cave were hanging upside down. All except one, who was hanging with his head upwards.
'What's the matter with him?' whispered one of the bats.
'Hush,' whispered the other. 'He's taken up yoga.'

Die Fledermäuse hingen mit dem Kopf nach unten in der Höhle; nur eine hing mit dem Kopf nach oben.
'Was ist los mit ihr?' fragte eine Fledermaus.
'Pst!—die hat den Yogafimmel.'

FRENCH	ITALIAN	SPANISH
Connaissez-vous l'histoire du ver luisant qui est mort en essayant de faire l'amour à un mégot allumé?	Avete sentito quella della povera lucciola che è morta per aver tentato di fare all'amore con una cicca accesa?	¿Sabes que hubo una luciérnaga que se murió tratando de hacerle el amor a una colilla?
Un fourreur et un expert-comptable allèrent en safari dans la jungle où ils s'enfoncèrent et se perdirent de plus en plus. La peur commença à les gagner. Tout à coup, ils entendirent un rugissement terrible et une bête gigantesque sauta sur le dos du fourreur. 'Pour l'amour du ciel,' hurla-t-il à son compagnon, 'qu'est-ce que c'est qu'cette bête qui est sur mon dos?' 'C'est pas à moi qu'il-faut demander,' répondit le comptable, 'c'est *toi* qui est fourreur, tu devrais le savoir!'	Un pellicciaio e un ragioniere che stavano esplorando la giungla si erano perduti ed erano terrorizzati. Con un terribile ruggito, un gigantesco animale piombò sulle spalle del pellicciaio. 'Per l'amore del cielo,' urlò quest'ultimo, 'che cos'è quell'affare sulle mie spalle?' 'Non chiederlo a me,' rispose il compagno. 'Sei *tu* il pellicciaio!'	Un peletero y un contable fueron de safari a la jungla, donde cada vez se perdían más y más y tenían más y más miedo. Hubo un terrible rugido y un gigantesco animal saltó a la espalda del peletero. —¡Santo Cielo! —gritó—. ¿Qué es lo que tengo en la espalda? —No me lo preguntes —respondió su amigo—. ¡El peletero eres tú!
Les chauves-souris étaient suspendues à la voûte de la grotte, la tête en bas. A l'exception d'une seule chauve-souris qui, elle, était suspendue la tête en haut. 'Qu'est-ce qu'elle a?' demanda une chauve-souris à sa voisine en chuchotant. 'Chut!' répondit l'autre, 'elle fait du yoga.'	I pipistrelli stavano appesi a testa in giú nella loro caverna. Solamente uno di loro stava con la testa all'insú. 'Che cosa gli è successo?' chiese uno dei pipistrelli. 'Sh. .' rispose un altro, 'sta facendo pratica di yoga.'	Los murciélagos se hallaban en su cueva, colgando del techo boca abajo. Todos menos uno, que colgaba con la cabeza hacia arriba. —¿Qué le pasa a éste? —susurró uno de los murciélagos. —¡Hum! —musitó el otro—. Está practicando yoga . . .

The lion met the little mouse.
'Who is the King of the Jungle?' asked the lion.
'You are,' said the mouse.
'That's right,' said the lion. 'And don't you forget it.'
So saying, he knocked the mouse down and kicked him against a tree.
A little later the lion met the chimpanzee.
'Who is the King of the Jungle?' asked the lion.
'You are,' said the chimpanzee.
'That's right,' said the lion. 'And don't you forget it.'
So saying, he knocked the chimpanzee down and stamped all over him.
The same thing happened with every animal the lion met.
Finally he met the elephant.
'Who is the King of the Jungle?' asked the lion.
The elephant picked up the lion with his trunk, dashed him to the ground, trampled all over him, sat on him, picked him up by the tail and battered him against a tree.
The lion staggered to his feet, bruised and bleeding, and said: 'I was only asking a civil question—Your Majesty.'

GERMAN

Ein Löwe trifft eine kleine Maus and fragt sie, wer der König des Dschungels ist.
'Du!' sagt die kleine Maus.
'Richtig,' sagt der Löwe, 'und merke es Dir gut!'
Mit diesen Worten gibt er der kleinen Maus einen Schlag mit seiner Pfote und schleudert sie gegen einen Baum.
Etwas später trifft der Löwe einen Schimpansen und fragt auch ihn:
'Wer ist der König des Dschungels?'
'Du!' sagt der Schimpanse.
'Richtig,' sagt der Löwe, 'und merke es Dir gut!'
Und mit diesen Worten schlug er den Schimpansen k.o.
So ging es mit jedem Tier, das seinen Weg kreuzte.
Schliesslich trifft der Löwe einen Elefanten.
'Wer ist der König des Dschungels?' fragt er ihn.
Der Elefant macht kurzen Prozess mit dem Löwen: mit seinem Rüssel ergreift er ihn, wirft ihn krachend nieder, trampelt über ihn, nimmt ihn dann beim Schwanz und schleudert ihn gegen einen Baum.
Schwankend, grün und blau rafft sich der Löwe wieder auf.
'Aber, das war doch eine ganz harmlose Frage, Königliche Hoheit!'

FRENCH

Le lion rencontra la souris.
'Qui est le Roi de la Jungle ?' demanda-t-il.
'C'est vous!' répondit la petite souris.
'Fort bien,' répliqua le lion, 'et tâche de ne pas l'oublier!'
Et sur ces mots, il assomma la souris d'un coup de patte et l'envoya s'écraser contre un arbre.
Un peu plus tard, le lion rencontra le chimpanzé.
'Qui est le Roi de la Jungle ?' lui demanda-t-il.
'C'est vous!' répondit le chimpanzé.
'Fort bien,' répliqua le lion, 'et tâche de ne pas l'oublier!'
Et sur ces mots, il assomma le chimpanzé d'un coup de patte et se mit à le piétiner.
La même scène se renouvela avec chacun des animaux que lion rencontra sur son passage.
Enfin, il recontra l'éléphant.
'Qui est le Roi de la Jungle ?' demanda le lion.
L'éléphant le saisit avec sa trompe, l'envoya rouler à terre, le piétina, s'assit de tout son poids sur lui, puis le prit par la queue et le balança contre un tronc d'arbre.
Le lion se releva en chancelant, meurtri et tout ensanglanté et dit: 'C'était une simple question de politesse, Votre Majesté!'

ITALIAN

Un leone incontrò un topolino.
'Chi è il re della giungla?' chiese il leone.
'Te,' rispose il topolino.
'Giusto,' disse il leone, 'e non lo dimenticare mai.'
Cosí dicendo afferrò il topo e lo scaraventò contro un albero.
Poco dopo il leone incontrò uno scimpanzé.
'Chi è il re della giungla?' chiese il leone.
'Te,' rispose lo scimpanzè.
'Giusto,' disse il leone, 'e non lo dimenticare mai.'
E cosí dicendo scaraventò lo scimpanzè a terra e lo calpestò. Lo stesso accadde a tutti gli animali con i quali il leone si imbattè.
Finalmente incontrò un elefante.
'Chi è il re della giungla?' chiese il leone.
L'elefante sollevò il leone con la proboscide, lo sbatacchiò a terra, lo calpestò, gli si sedette sopra, lo tirò su per la coda e lo scaraventò contro un albero.
Rialzandosi in piedi a fatica, illividito e sanguinante, il leone disse: 'Maestà, io non avevo fatto che una domanda.'

SPANISH

El león se encontró con el ratoncito.
—¿Quién es el rey de la selva? —preguntó el león.
—Tu eres el rey —respondió el ratoncito.
—Eso está bien —dijo el león—. !Y no lo olvides!
Y diciendo esto le dió un manotazo y lo tiró contra un árbol.
Poco después el león encontró a un chimpancé.
—¿Quién es el rey de la selva? —volvió a preguntar.
—Tu eres el rey —dijo el chimpancé.
—Eso está bien —repuso el león—. ¡¡Y no lo olvides!
Y diciéndolo le dio un manotazo que le hizo volar por los aires.
Lo mismo ocurrió con los demás animales que el león encontró a su paso.
Hasta que al fin se acercó al elefante.
—¿Quién es el rey de la selva —preguntó el león.
El elefante agarró al león con la trompa, lo derribó al suelo, lo pataleó, se le sentó encima y cogiéndolo por la cola lo estrelló contra un árbol.
El león se levantó como pudo, doliente y sangrando, y dijo:
—¡Sólo era una pregunta formularia, Su Majestad!

GERMAN

The boy and girl rabbit were chased by two foxes. They dived into a hole to escape, leaving the foxes outside. Two hours later the foxes were still waiting. 'What on earth can we do?' said the girl rabbit. 'There's no other way out of this hole.'
'Don't worry,' said the boy rabbit. 'Let's just stay here until we outnumber them.'

Der Kaninchenjunge und seine Freundin wurden von zwei Füchsen gejagd. Sie retteten sich in letzter Sekunde in ein Erdloch. Die Füchse standen draussen und warteten. Nach zwei Stunden etwa fragte das Kaninchenmädchen verzweifelt:
'Was sollen wir nur machen? Es gibt ja nur einen Ausgang!'
'Du brauchst keine Angst zu haben,' tröstete sie der Kaninchenjunge; 'wir bleiben einfach solange hier, bis wir ihnen zahlenmässig überlegen sind.'

The two explorers were going through the jungle when a ferocious-looking lion appeared on the track in front of them.
'Keep calm,' said the first explorer. 'Remember what we read in that book on wild animals? If you stand absolutely still and look a lion straight in the eye, he will turn tail and run away.'
'Fine,' said the second explorer. 'You've read the book. I've read the book. But has *he* read the book?'

Zwei Forscher bahnten ihren Weg durch den Urwald.
Plötzlich stand ein gefährlicher Löwe vor ihnen.
'Nur nicht die Nerven verlieren!' sagte der eine Froscher, 'das Buch, das wir gelesen haben, gab uns ja Verhaltungsmassregeln für solche Situationen: man muss still stehen bleiben, dem Löwen gerade in die Augen sehen—dann macht er kehrt und läuft davon.'
'Alles gut und schön . . . Du hast das Buch gelesen, ich habe es gelesen . . . aber hat der Löwe es gelesen?'

FRENCH	ITALIAN	SPANISH
Le petit lapin et la petite lapine étaient poursuivis par deux renards. Ils plongèrent dans un étroit terrier pour échapper à leurs poursuivants. Deux heures plus tard, les deux renards attendaient toujours dehors, à l'entrée du terrier. 'Mon Dieu! Que va-t-on faire?' demanda la petite lapine. 'Il n'y a pas d'autre sortie.' 'T'inquiète pas,' dit le lapin; 'on va rester ici jusqu'à ce que nous soyions dix fois plus nombreux qu'eux.'	Il coniglio e la sua compagna erano stati inseguiti da due volpi. Si gettarono in un buco per salvarsi, lasciando fuori le volpi. Due ore dopo, le volpi erano ancora all'agguato. 'Che diamine facciamo ora?' disse la coniglia, 'non c'è altra uscita da questo buco.' 'Non stare a preoccuparti,' disse il coniglio, 'rimarremo qui fintanto che saremo in piú di loro.'	Un conejo y una coneja eran perseguidos por dos zorras. Para escapar se metieron en una madriguera, dejando a la zorra en el exterior. Pero dos horas después las zorras se encontraban aún vigilando. —¿Qué haremos? —dijo la coneja—. Esta madriguera no tiene otra salida. —No te apures —contestó el conejo—. Nos quedaremos aquí hasta que les genemos en número.
Deux explorateurs s'avançaient dans la jungle lorsqu'apparut devant eux sur le sentier un lion à l'aspect féroce. 'Garde ton sang-froid,' dit l'un d'eux à l'autre. 'Tu te rappelles c'qu'on a lu dans ce livre sur les bêtes sauvages? Si on reste absolument immobile en regardant le lion droit dans les yeux, il nous tournera le dos et partira comme il est venu.' 'Très bien,' répliqua l'autre explorateur. 'Tu as lu le bouquin; je l'ai lu moi aussi mais est-ce qu'il l'a lu, *lui*?'	Due esploratori stavano attraversando la giungla quando un feroce leone si parò loro davanti. 'Sta calmo,' disse il primo esploratore. 'Ricordi che cosa abbiamo letto in quel libro sugli animali selvaggi? Se ti mantieni perfettamente fermo e guardi il leone fisso negli occhi, egli si volterà indietro e fuggirà.' 'Giusto,' disse il secondo esploratore, 'tu hai letto il libro, io l'ho letto, ma chi sa se *lui* l'ha letto?'	Dos exploradores iban por la selva cuando un león de aspecto feroz se plantó enfrente de ellos, en el camino. —Ten calma —dijo un explorador—. ¿Recuerdas lo que leímos en aquel libro sobre los animales salvajes? Si te quedas completamente inmóvil, mirando al león en los ojos, éste da media vuelta y se va. —¡Magnífico! —dijo el otro—. Tu has leido el libro; yo lo he leido también. Pero, y el león, ¿lo ha leido?

OUR DUMB FRIENDS

GERMAN

The scientist went out to the Arizona Desert to discover why the coyotes howled. After months of research, he was still baffled. He was about to give up in despair, when he met an old prospector. As a last, desperate effort he asked the prospector if he knew why the coyotes howled.
'Easy,' said the grizzled old man. 'Out in the desert there ain't no trees—jest cactus.'

Ein Forscher verbrachte Monate in der Einöde von Arizona, um herauszufinden, warum der Steppenwolf heult, und sah sich bereits am Ende seiner Mühe. Da traf er einen Schürfer und er fragte ihn, ob er die Antwort auf seine Frage hätte.
'Natürlich,' sagte der Mann, 'das ist doch ganz einfach: weil es hier nur Kakteen gibt und keine Bäume.'

ANYTHING GOES

The Arab was riding on his camel through the remotest part of the desert when he met a man dressed in full skin-diving equipment—flippers, mask, oxygen cylinder, and harpoon-gun.
'Pardon me,' said the skin-diver. 'Could you tell me how far it is to the sea?'
'About seven hundred miles,' said the Arab.
'In that case,' said the skin-diver, 'I'll wait until the tide comes in.'

Ein Beduin ritt auf seinem Kamel durch die Wüste.
Er begegnete einem Mann, der Schwimmflossen, Sauerstoffmaske und Harpune trug.
'Können Sie mir sagen, wie weit es bis zum Meer ist?'
'Etwa siebenhundert Meilen,' sagte der Beduin.
'O!—dann ist es wohl besser, wenn ich hier warte, bis die Flut wieder reinkommt.'

FRENCH

Un savant décida d'aller dans le désert de l'Arizona pour découvrir ce qui faisait hurler les coyotes. Après des mois de recherches, il n'était pas plus avancé qu'au commencement.

Il était sur le point de tout lâcher, en désespoir de cause, lorsqu'il rencontra un vieux chercheur d'or. A tout hasard, il lui demanda s'il savait pourquoi les coyotes hurlaient.

'C'est très simple,' répondit le vieil homme. 'Y a pas d'arbre dans ce désert; y a que du cactus!'

ITALIAN

Uno scienziato si recò nel deserto dell'Arizona per scoprire perché i cani di prateria ululano. Dopo mesi di ricerche, ne sapeva quanto prima. In disperazione era sul punto di abbandonare le ricerche, quando incontrò un vecchio esploratore. Come ultima, disperata speranza, gli chiese se sapeva perché i cani di prateria ululano.

'È ovvio,' disse il vecchio, 'là nel deserto non ci sono alberi—soltanto dei cacti.'

SPANISH

El científico se marchó al desierto de Arizona para averiguar porqué los coyotes aúllan. Después de varios meses de estudio, nada había conseguido. Se hallaba ya al borde de la desesperación cuando se encontró con un viejo explorador. Como un último y desesperado intento le preguntó si sabía porque aullaban los coyotes.

—¡Claro! —dijo el viejo—. En este desierto no hay árboles . . . todo son cactus.

Un Arabe traversait à dos de chameau une région particulièrement lointaine et aride du désert lorsqu'il rencontra un homme en combinaison de caoutchouc et tout le matériel de plongée sous-marine: palmes, lunettes de plongée, cylindre d'oxygène et harpon.

'Excusez-moi,' dit ce dernier, 'pouvez-vous me dire si on est loin de la mer?'

'Environ mille kilomètres,' répondit l'Arabe.

'Auquel cas,' dit le chasseur sous-marin, 'j'attendrai ici que la marée remonte.'

Un Arabo stava attraversando sul suo cammello una delle parti più remote del deserto, quando incontrò un uomo in completa tenuta da sommozzatore—pinne, maschera, cilindro di ossigeno e fiocina.

'Mi scusi,' disse il sommozzatore. 'Mi sa dire quanto dista il mare?'

'Circa settecento miglia,' rispose l'Arabo.

'Allora,' disse il sommozzatore, 'mi conviene aspettare che si alzi la marea.'

Un árabe montaba su camello por el más remoto lugar del desierto, cuando se tropezó con un hombre equipado con traje de inmersión completo: aletas, careta, tubos de oxígeno y un fusil de pesca submarina.

—Perdone —dijo el buceador—, ¿podría decirme si está muy lejos el mar?

—A unas setecientas millas —contestó el árabe.

—En este caso —repuso el buceador—, me quedaré aquí hasta que suba la marea.

GERMAN

The revolutionary was standing, blindfolded, facing the firing squad.
'Any last request?' asked the officer in charge.
'Yes,' said the revolutionary. 'I'd like to see my mother.'
'And where is your mother?'
'In Australia.'

Der Revolutionär stand bereits mit verbundenen Augen vor dem Hinrichtungskommando, als ihn der diensthabende Offizier fragte:
'Haben Sie einen letzten Wunsch?'
'Ja, ich möchte meine Mutter sehen.'
'Wo ist Ihre Mutter?'
'In Australien.'

'It's sheer victimisation,' said the night watchman who had just been dismissed from his job. 'I was fired for talking on duty.'
'Just for talking?' said his friend.
'Well,' said the nightwatchman, 'just for talking in my sleep.'

'Solche Gemeinheit,' sagte der Nachtwächter, 'mich rauszuschmeissen, nur weil ich im Dienst gesprochen habe!'
'Das ist aber wirklich kein Grund,' sagte sein Freund.
'Und ich wusste gar nichts davon—ich habe im Schlaf gesprochen.'

The guests had overstayed their welcome at the dinner party. Mr Bristow, yawning as they made their farewells, shook hands and said: 'I'll be glad to see you again . . . whenever you've less time to spare.'

Die Gäste blieben nach dem Abendessen noch stundenlang.
Als sie sich schliesslich verabschiedeten, sagte der Gastgeber gähnend:
'Kommen Sie bald wieder, wenn Sie weniger Zeit haben.'

FRENCH

Le révolutionnaire attendait, les yeux bandés, face au peloton d'exécution.
'Avez-vous un dernier souhait à formuler?' demanda l'officier.
'Oui!' répondit le révolutionnaire. 'J'aimerais voir ma mère.'
'Et où vit-elle?'
'En Australie.'

ITALIAN

Il rivoluzionario stava, bendato, davanti al plotone di esecuzione.
'Avete un'ultimo desiderio? gli chiese il comandante.
'Si,' disse il rivoluzionario. 'Vorrei vedere mia madre.'
'E dov'è vostra madre?'
'In Australia.'

SPANISH

El revolucionario, con los ojos vendados, se hallaba ya dispuesto frente el piquete de ejecución.
—¿Algún último deseo? —le preguntó el oficial.
—Sí . . . —dijo el revolucionario—. Quiero ver a mi madre.
—Y, ¿dónde está su madre?
—En Australia.

'C'est de la persécution,' se lamenta le gardien de nuit qui venait de se faire mettre à la porte. 'J'ai été foutu à la porte rien que pour avoir parlé pendant le travail!'
'Quoi? Juste pour avoir parlé?' demanda son ami.
'Ouais,' répondit le gardien de nuit, 'juste pour avoir parlé dans mon sommeil.'

'È il colmo dell'ingiustizia,' disse il guardiano notturno che aveva appena perso il suo posto. 'Mi hanno licenziato perché parlavo mentre ero di guardia.'
'Solo perché parlavi?' gli chiese un amico.
'Be',' disse il guardiano, 'solo perché parlavo nel sonno.'

—¡Soy una víctima! —decía el vigilante nocturno que acababa de ser despedido del trabajo—. Me han echado por hablar estando de servicio.
—¿Sólo por hablar? —preguntó su amigo.
—Bueno . . . —repuso el vigilante—. ¡Por hablar en sueños!

Les invités à dîner s'étaient attardés outre mesure chez leur hôte, M. Bristow.
Baillant largement au moment de leur départ, celui-ci leur serra la main en disant:
'Je serais heureux de vous revoir encore, quand vous aurez moins de temps à perdre.'

Gli ospiti si erano attardati un po' troppo a lungo dopo cena. Mr Bristow, sbadigliando mentre li salutava, strinse loro la mano e disse:
'Sarò felice di rivedervi . . . quando avete un po' meno tempo a vostra disposizione.'

Los invitados habían prolongado su estancia después de la cena. El señor Bristow, bostezando mientras les despedía, les tendió la mano y dijo:
—Me será muy grato recibirles de nuevo . . . cuando tengan menos tiempo que perder.

ANYTHING GOES

GERMAN

The toothless policeman was giving evidence against O'Rafferty.
'The accused kicked me in the mouth, knocking out all my teeth, your honour.'
'It's a lie!' shouted O'Rafferty from the dock. 'He bit me!'
'The officer bit you?' said the judge. 'And where exactly did he bite you?'
'On the toe of me right boot, your honour.'

Zahnlos machte der Polizist seine Aussage gegen O'Rafferty.
'Dann trat der Angeklagte mit seinem Fuss meine Zähne aus.'
'Das ist gelogen!' schrie O'Rafferty von der Anklagebank.
'Er hat sich die Zähne an mir ausgebissen!'
'Hat der Polizeibeamte Sie gebissen?' fragte der Richter erstaunt.
'Ja, Euer Würden, durch meine rechte Stiefelspitze!'

WOMEN

'Mavis can't keep a secret,' said the woman to her friend. 'She told me that you told her something I told you not to tell her.'
'Mavis is completely untrustworthy,' said the friend. 'I told her not to tell you that I told her something you told me not to tell her.'
'Disgraceful,' said the first woman.
'Don't ever tell her that I told you that she told me that you told her something I told you not to tell her.'

'Mavis kann nichts für sich behalten,' sagt die Freundin zur Freundin. 'Sie hat mir gesagt, Du hättest ihr etwas gesagt, was ich Dir gesagt habe, und was Du ihr nicht weitersagen solltest.'
'Ach, man kann Mavis doch nicht trauen! Ich habe ihr extra gesagt, sie soll Dir nicht sagen, dass ich ihr gesagt habe was Du mir gesagt hast und was ich ihr nicht weitersagen sollte.'
'Ja, sie ist wirklich schrecklich,' sagt die Freundin zur Freundin. 'Sag' ihr bitte nie, dass ich Dir gesagt habe, dass sie mir gesagt hat, dass Du ihr gesagt hast, was ich Dir gesagt habe und was Du ihr nicht weitersagen solltest!'

FRENCH	ITALIAN	SPANISH
L'agent de police édenté témoignait au tribunal contre O'Rafferty. 'Monsieur le Président, l'accusé m'a donné un coup de pied au visage qui m'a cassé toutes mes dents.' 'C'est pas vrai!' hurla O'Rafferty de la barre. 'C'est lui qui m'a mordu!' 'L'officier de paix vous a mordu?' demanda le juge; 'et où exactement vous a-t-il mordu?' 'Au pied, à l'endroit du gros orteil, M'sieur le Président.'	Un poliziotto tutto sdentato stava deponendo contro O'Rafferty. 'L'accusato mi ha dato un calcio in bocca, facendomi cascare tutti i denti.' 'È una bugia!' gridò O'Rafferty dal banco degli imputati. 'È lui che mi ha dato un morso.' 'L'agente vi ha morso?' disse il giudice. 'E dove?' 'Sulla punta dello stivale destro, eccellenza.'	El policía, sin dientes, declaraba contra O'Rafferty. —El acusado me golpeó en la boca y me rompió los dientes, Su Señoría. —¡Mentira! —esclamó O'Rafferty desde el banquillo—. ¡El me mordió! —¿Que el oficial le mordió? —interpeló el juez—. ¿Y en qué lugar le mordió, exactamente? —En la punta de mi zapato derecho, Su Señoría.
'Mavis est incapable de garder un secret,' dit la femme à son amie. 'Elle m'a dit que tu lui as dit quelque chose que je t'avais dit de ne pas lui dire.' 'On peut vraiment pas faire confiance à Mavis!' déclara l'amie. 'J'lui avais bien dit pourtant de ne pas te dire que je lui avais dit quelque chose que tu m'as dit de ne pas lui dire.' 'C'est dégueulasse!' s'écria la première, 'ne lui dis jamais que je t'ai dit qu'elle m'a dit que tu lui as dit quelque chose que je t'ai dit de ne pas lui dire!'	'Mavis non sa tenere un segreto,' disse una donna all'amica. 'Mi ha detto che tu le hai detto qualche cosa che ti avevo detto io dicendote di non dirglielo.' 'Non ci si può proprio fidare di Mavis,' rispose l'amica. 'Io le ho detto di non dirti che le avevo detto una cosa che tu mi avevi detto di non dirle.' 'Che vergogna!' disse la prima donna. 'Ora mi raccomando di non dirle che io ti ho detto che lei mi ha detto che tu lei hai detto una cosa che io ti avevo detto di non dirle.'	—Mavis no sabe guardar un secreto —decía una mujer a su amiga—. Me dijo que tu le dijiste algo que yo te había dicho que no le dijeras. —Mavis es completamente indigna de confianza —contestó la amiga—. Yo le dije que no te dijera que yo le había dicho algo que tú me dijiste que no le dijera. —¡Es vergonzoso! —repuso la primera mujer—. ¡No le digas nunca que yo te dije que ella me ha dicho que tu le dijiste algo que yo te había dicho que no le dijeras!

WOMEN

GERMAN

Fat Ethel sat down at the lunch counter and ordered a whole fruit cake. 'Shall I cut it into four pieces or eight?' asked the waitress. 'Four,' said Ethel. 'I'm on a diet.'	Die dicke Ethel sitzt im Café und bestellt sich einen ganzen Kuchen. 'Soll ich ihn in acht Teile schneiden?' fragt die Kellnerin. 'Nein, bitte in vier, ich muss dünner werden.'
Eve was running her fingers over Adam's ribs one day, and discovered he had two missing. 'Own up,' she said: 'Who's the other woman?'	Als Eva einmal wieder ihre Finger über Adams Rippen laufen liess, bemerkte sie, dass zwei fehlten. 'Raus mit der Sprache,' sagte sie, 'wer ist die andere?'
If a woman's intuition is as good as they say, why must they keep on asking questions?	Ist Intuition der Frauen wirklich so gut? Warum fragen sie dann immer noch so viel?

MISCELLANEOUS

O'Rafferty had come back from a Mediterranean cruise and had died. His friend Flynn called to pay his respects. 'Poor ould fella,' said Flynn to the widow as he looked down at the suntanned corpse in the coffin. 'But ye must admit—his holiday did him the power of good.'	O'Rafferty kam von einer Mittelmeer-Reise zurück und starb. Sein Freund Flynn machte einen Beileidsbesuch bei der Witwe. 'Der arme Kerl,' sagte er, als er den braungebrannten Körper im Sarg liegen sah. 'Aber Sie müssen zugeben, dieser Urlaub hat ihm sehr gutgetan.'

FRENCH	ITALIAN	SPANISH
La grosse Ethel s'assit au restaurant et commanda une tarte anx fruits entière. 'Voulez-vous que je la coupe en quatre ou en huit?' demanda la serveuse. 'En quatre, seulement,' répondit Ethel, 'je suis au régime.'	Una grassona prese il posto ad un bar e ordinò un' intera torta di frutta. 'Devo tagliarla in quattro porzioni o in otto?' chiese la cameriera. 'In quattro,' sospirò la grassona. 'Sono a dieta.'	Pat Ethel se sentó en el mostrador y pidió un pastel de fruta entero. —¿Se lo corto en cuatro trozos o en ocho? —le preguntó la camarera. —En cuatro —dijo Ethel—. ¡Estoy a régimen!
Un jour qu'Eve caressait du doigt la poitrine d'Adam, elle remarqua qu'il lui manquait deux côtes. 'Allez, pas de cachoteries!' dit-elle, 'qui est l'autre?'	Un giorno mentre carezzava le costole di Adamo, Eva si accorse che gliene mancavano due. 'Non ingannarmi,' disse, 'chi è l'altra donna?'	Un día, Eva recorría con los dedos las costillas de Adán y descubrió que le faltaban dos. —¡Anda, confiésalo! —dijo—. ¿Quién la otra mujer?
Si l'intuition féminine est aussi sûre que les femmes voudraient le faire croire, alors pourquoi posent-elles des questions?	Se esiste veramente questo famoso intuito femminile, perché le donne fanno sempre tante domande?	Si la intuición femenina es tan buena como dicen, ¿por qué tienen que estar continuamente haciendo preguntas?
O'Rafferty revenait d'une croisière en Méditerranée lorsqu'il mourut. Son ami Flynn alla faire ses condoléances à la veuve. 'Pauvre gars,' dit-il à la veuve en regardant le corps bronzé de son ami gisant dans le cercueil. 'Et pourtant, y a pas à dire, c'est fou ce qu'elle lui a fait du bien cette croisière!'	Di ritorno da una crociera nel Mediterraneo, O'Rafferty morí. Il suo amico Flynn passò a rendere l'ultimo omaggio alla salma. 'Pover'uomo!' mormorò alla vedova, guardando il volto abbronzato dell'amico adagiato nel feretro. 'Ma bisogna riconoscere che la vacanza gli ha fatto proprio bene.'	O'Rafferty acababa de regresar de un crucero por el Mediterráneo cuando se murió. Su amigo Flynn acudió a dar el pésame. —¡Pobre amigo mío! —le dijo Flynn a la viuda, mientras contemplaba el rostro curtido por el sol que yacía en el ataud—. ¡No se puede negar que estas vacaciones le han dado un aspecto saludable!

GERMAN

Mad Harry was building a fence. Every so often he would mutter in disgust and throw some of the nails away.
Silly Fred was watching. Eventually, he could contain his curiosity no longer.
'Why do you keep throwing those nails away?' asked Fred.
'Because they're no use,' snapped Harry. 'Half of them have the points on the wrong end.'
Silly Fred picked up a few nails and examined them carefully.
'You idiot!' he exclaimed. 'These are for the other side of the fence.'

Der blöde Harry baut einen Lattenzaun. Hin und wieder unterbricht er seine Hämmerei, schimpft verärgert und wirft einen Nagel weg. Sein Freund Fred sieht sich das eine Weile an und fragt dann schliesslich:
'Warum wirfst Du denn die vielen Nägel weg?'
'Weil sie unbrauchbar sind —sie haben alle den Kopf am falschen Ende,' sagt Harry ungeduldig.
Fred hebt einige Nägel auf, untersucht sie sehr sorgfältig und sagt dann schliesslich:
'Bist Du ein Idiot! Diese Nägel sind für die andere Seite der Latten bestimmt!'

There was the stage hypnotist who committed suicide through sheer frustration. The better his act, the fewer people were left awake to applaud.

Aus reiner Verzweiflung nahm sich der Hypnotiseur das Leben: seine Darbietungen wuerden immer besser und der Applaus immer dünner. Einer nach dem andern schlief ein.

Smith was called into the boss's office.
'You're lucky, Smith,' snarled the boss. 'We were going to replace you with a machine. But we've not been able to find out yet what you do all day.'

Smith wurde zum Chef gerufen.
'Haben Sie ein Glück, Smith,' sagte er kochend, 'wir wollten Ihre Arbeit in Zukunft von einer Maschine machen lassen, aber es ist uns leider nicht klar, was Sie den ganzen Tag machen.'

FRENCH	ITALIAN	SPANISH
Harry le Fol était en train d'élever une barrière. De temps en temps, on l'entendait marmonner entre ses dents sur un ton dégoûté et jeter des clous par terre. Fred le Simple l'observait. Enfin, ne pouvant plus contenir sa curiosité, il demanda: 'Pourquois jettes-tu ces clous?' 'Parce qu'ils sont bons à rien!' rétorqua Harry d'un ton rageur. 'La moitié de ces clous sont pointus du mauvais côté.' Fred le Simple ramassa quelques uns et les examina soigneusement. 'Idiot!' s'exclama-t-il. 'Ces clous là, ils sont pour l'autre côté de la barrière!'	Harry il matto stava erigendo una palizzata. Ogni tanto sbofonchiava qualche cosa e gettava via delle manciate di chiodi. Fred lo stupido stava ad osservarlo. Ad un tratto non poté piú contenere la sua curiosità: 'Mi spieghi perché continui a buttare via i chiodi?' 'Perché non servono,' rispose Harry. 'Almeno la metà ha la punta dalla parte sbagliata.' Fred raccolse alcuni chiodi e li osservò attentamente. 'Idiota!' esclamò. 'Questi servono per l'altra parte della staccionata.'	El tonto de Harry levantaba una valla. De vez en cuando gruñía con disgusto y arrojaba algunos clavos. El tonto de Fred lo contemplaba. Y de pronto no pudo contener por más tiempo su curiosidad. —¿Por qué tiras esos clavos? —preguntó Fred. —Porque no sirven —exclamó Harry—. La mitad de ellos tienen la punta en el otro extremo. El tonto de Fred recogió algunos clavos y los examinó cuidadosamente. —¡Idiota! —exclamó al fin—. ¡Estos clavos son para el otro lado de la valla!
En désespoir de cause, un hypnotiseur finit par se suicider. En effet, plus son numéro était réussi et moins il restait de spectateurs assez éveillés pour l'applaudir.	C'era una volta un ipnotizzatore da varietà che, in preda a un senso di frustrazione, finí per suicidarsi. Meglio riusciva il suo numero e meno erano gli spettatori rimasti svegli per applaudire.	Había un hipnotista de teatro que se suicidaba de pura frustración. Pero cuando mejor era su actuación, menos era el público que permanecía despierto para aplaudirle.
Smith fut appelé au bureau du patron. 'Vous avez de la chance, Smith!' ricana celui-ci. 'On va mettre une machine à votre place, mais on n'a pas encore été foutu de savoir c'que vous faites toute la journée.'	Smith viene chiamato a rapporto nell'ufficio del Capo. 'Sei fortunato, Smith,' borbotta questi. 'Intendevamo rimpiazzarti con una macchina, ma ancora non siamo riusciti a scoprire che diavolo fai tutto il giorno.'	A Smith le llamaron al despacho del jefe. —Está de suerte, Smith —le dijo el jefe—. Vamos a sustituirle por una máquina. Pero aún no se nos ha ocurrido qué es lo que hará usted en todo el día.

GERMAN

The painters were working slowly away at the big room. All except one, who new to the job, was painting at great speed. The foreman, unused to such energy from his workmen, stopped the painter. 'I'm proud of you, lad,' he said. 'You're really showing the others how to work.'
'It's not that,' said the new man: 'I haven't got as much paint as the others, and I'm trying to finish before it runs out.'

Die Anstreicher nahmen sich Zeit mit der Arbeit. Nur einer, der jüngste, malte eifrig drauflos.
Den Vorarbeiter überraschte das sehr. Er unterbrach den Jungen und sagte:
'So ist es recht, mein Junge, Du zeigst es den andern, wie man zu arbeiten hat.'
'Das ist es nicht. Ich habe nur weniger Farbe als sie; ich beeile mich, damit sie aus reicht, bis ich mit der Arbeit fertig bin.'

His mother-in-law had died, and Smith was making the funeral arrangements. 'Would you like her buried, cremated or embalmed?' asked the undertaker.
'All three,' said Smith. 'I'm taking no chances.'

Die Schwiegermutter ist gestorben und Smith kümmert sich um das Begräbnis. Der Leichenbestatter fragt, ob sie begraben, eingeäschert oder einbalsamiert werden soll.

'Machen Sie alles,' sagt Smith, 'sicher ist sicher.'

What must a man be to receive a state funeral?
Dead.

Was muss ein Mann tun, um ein Staatsbegräbnis zu bekommen?
Sterben.

FRENCH	ITALIAN	SPANISH
Les ouvriers-peintres ne se pressaient pas pour finir la grande pièce. Tous à l'exception d'un seul, qui était nouveau dans le métier et qui maniait le pinceau avec enthousiasme. Nullement habitué à un tel déploiement d'énergie de la part de ses ouvriers, le contremaître l'interrompit dans son travail et lui dit: 'Je suis fier de toi, mon garçon! Voilà c'que j'appelle montrer aux autres comment il faut travailler!' 'C'est pas du tout ça,' répondit le nouveau, 'j'ai pas autant de peinture que les autres et c'est pour ça que j'essaie de finir le boulot avant qu'il n'en reste plus.'	Degli imbianchini stavano pitturando le pareti di una grande stanza molto lentamente. Tutti ad eccezione di uno che, nuovo al mestiere, dipingeva con grande alacrità. Il caposquadra, sorpreso da tanta energia, lo fermò. 'Sono orgoglioso di te, ragazzo,' disse, 'stai proprio dando un buon esempio agli altri.' 'No, non è per quello,' disse il ragazzo, 'è che ho meno vernice degli altri e sto cercando di terminare il lavoro prima che finisca la vernice.'	Los pintores trabajaban despacio en la gran habitación. Todos menos uno, nuevo en el oficio, que pintaba a toda velocidad. El encargado, poco habituado a ver tanta energía en sus operarios, se acercó al pintor. —Estoy satisfecho de ti, muchacho —le dijo—. Estás demostrándoles a todos como se trabaja. —No es eso —respondió el novato—. Es que me han dado menos pintura que a los demás, y trato de acabar antes de que se me termine.
Sa belle-mère était morte et Smith s'était chargé d'organiser les funérailles. 'Désirez-vous un enterrement, une crémation ou un embaumement? demanda l'entrepreneur des pompes funèbres. 'Je veux tout ça à la fois,' répondit Smith, 'au moins ainsi je suis sûr d'être tranquille!'	La suocera di Smith era morta, e Smith stava dando disposizioni per i funerali. 'Dobbiamo seppellirla, cremarla o imbalsamarla?' chiese l'impresario delle pompe funebri. 'Tutt'e tre,' rispose Smith. 'Non voglio davvero correre rischi.'	Su suegra acababa de morir, y Smith realizaba los trámites para el sepelio. —¿Quiere que la enterremos, que la incineremos o que la embalsamemos? —le preguntó el de la funeraria. —Las tres cosas a la vez —contestó Smith—. ¡No voy a correr el riesgo!
Que faut-il faire pour recevoir des funérailles nationales? Mourir!	Che cosa bisogna essere per meritarsi un funerale di stato? Morti.	—¿Qué se necesita para que le hagan a uno un funeral de lujo? —Estar muerto.

GERMAN

The co-pilot came out of the plane's cockpit.
'Does anyone here believe in the life hereafter?' he asked.
'I do! I do!' shouted an intense, bespectacled young man.
'Good,' said the co-pilot. 'We're about to crash and we're a parachute short.'

Der Pilot kommt aus der Kanzel und fragt die Passagiere:
'Ist jemand unter Ihnen, der an ein Leben nach dem Tode glaubt?'
'Ja, ich,' sagte ein scheuer junger Mann mit Brille.
'Das ist gut,' sagte der Pilot. 'Wir stürzen nämlich gleich ab und uns fehlt ein Fallschirm.'

The retired British colonel was telling a long-haired, with-it youth the story of how he won his Victoria Cross.

'There I was,' he said, 'surrounded by hostile natives. They hit me over the head with clubs, then pinned me to the ground with spears. I had spears through my arms, through my legs and through my chest. Then they covered me with brushwood and set fire to me.'
'Did it hurt?' sneered the long-haired youth, sarcastically.
'Only when I laughed.'

Ein britischer Oberst a.D. erzählt einem langhaarigen Jüngling wie er sich sein Viktoria Kreuz verdient hat:
'Ich war umringt von feindseligen Eingeborenen. Sie schlugen mit Knüppel auf mich ein, nagelten mich mit ihren Speeren durch Arme, Brust und Beine auf den Boden, warfen Reisig über mich und setzten das Zeug in Brand.'
'Hat es wehgetan?' fragte der Langhaarige sarkastisch.
'Nur beim Lachen,' sagte der Oberst.

FRENCH | **ITALIAN** | **SPANISH**

FRENCH

Le co-pilote sortit du poste de pilotage de l'avion de ligne.
'Y a-t-il ici quelqu'un qui croit en la vie outre-tombe?' demanda-t-il aux passagers.
'Moi j'y crois!' s'écria un jeune homme à lunettes et au visage intense.
'Bon,' répondit le co-pilote, 'c'est très bien, car nous allons bientôt nous écraser au sol et il nous manque un parachute.'

ITALIAN

Il secondo pilota uscí dalla carlinga.
'C'è qualcuno fra voi che crede nella vita eterna?' domandò.
'Io ci credo,' esclamò con ardore un giovane occhialuto.
'Meno male!' disse il pilota.
'L'aereo sta per precipitare e ci manca un paracadute.'

SPANISH

El copiloto salió de la cabina del avión.
—¿Hay alguien aquí que crea en la vida futura? —preguntó.
—¡Yo creo, yo creo! —exclamó con vehemencia un joven con gafas.
—¡Estupendo! —repuso el copiloto—. Vamos a estrellarnos y nos falta un paracaídas.

FRENCH

Le colonel retraité de l'armée britannique racontait à un jeune homme moderne et tout (cheveux longs, idées de gauche, tout ce qu'il y a de plus dans le vent) comment il avait gagné la Victoria Cross.
'Je me suis trouvé donc,' dit-il, 'complètement entouré par une foule d'indigènes hostiles qui se mirent à m'assommer à coups de gourdin sur le crâne et finirent par me clouer au sol avec leurs lances. J'en avais qui me traversaient les bras, la poitrine, les jambes, partout . . . Puis ils m'ont couvert de branches et y mirent le feu.'
'Ça vous a fait mal?' demanda le jeune chevelu. sarcastique.
'Pas vraiment, sauf quand je me suis mis à rire.'

ITALIAN

Un colonnello inglese a riposo stava raccontando ad un giovane capellone la storia di come si era conquistato la medaglia d'oro:
'Ed io me ne stavo là, circondanto dagli indigeni ribelli. Mi percossero con i randelli, poi con le lance, mi trafissero le braccia, le gambe ed il petto. Mi cosparsero di segatura e vi appiccarono il fuoco.'
'E le faceva male?' domandò con sarcasmo il giovane capellone.
'Solamente se ridevo.'

SPANISH

Un coronel inglés retirado le explicaba a un joven melenudo la historia de cómo había ganado su Cruz Victoria.
—Allí estaba —decía—, rodeado de nativos hostiles. Me golpearon con palos en la cabeza y me clavaron al suelo con sus lanzas. Tenía lanzas en los brazos, en las piernas y en el pecho. Entonces me cubrieron con maleza y le prendieron fuego.
—¿Y dolía? —le preguntó el melenudo sarcásticamente.
—Sólo cuando me reía.

GERMAN

The circus performer used to dive 50 feet into a wet sponge. One day he broke his neck. Someone had wrung out the sponge.

Täglich machte der Mann im Zirkus seinen 20-Meter 'Todessprung' in einen nassen Schwamm. Eines Tages brach er sich das Genick. Jemand hatte den Schwamm ausgedrückt.

Carruthers was a gambling man, putting money wherever he could on horses, dogs, football pools, dice, dominoes or card games. One day he was playing cards with Forsyth, when Forsyth dropped dead. Carruthers had the job of breaking the news to Mrs Forsyth. She answered the ring at her doorbell. 'Excuse me,' said Carruthers, 'but are you the widow Forsyth?'
'I'm not a widow.'
'Would you care to make a little bet?'

Carruthers konnte das Wetten nicht lassen. Überall legte er Geld an: Pferde, Hunde, Fussballtoto, Würfel, Karten.
Eines Tages spielte er mit Forsyth Karten, als dieser plötzlich tot vom Stuhl fiel. Nun musste Carruthers die traurige Nachricht Mrs Forsyth bringen.
Er klingelt. Sie kommt zur Tür.
'Verzeihung, sind Sie Forsyth' Witwe?'
'Was sollen die dummen Witze! Ich bin keine Witwe,' sagte Mrs Forsyth irritiert.
'Was wollen Sie wetten?'

The Chinaman was asked his opinion of Europeans. 'I honestly don't know,' he said. 'They all look alike to me.'

Der Chinese, über seinen Eindruck von den Europäern befragt:
'Schwer zu sagen, sie sehen ja alle gleich aus'.

FRENCH	ITALIAN	SPANISH
L'acrobate de cirque plongeait tête première d'une hauteur de 15 mètres sur une éponge mouillée. Puis, un jour il se cassa le cou. Quelqu'un avait essoré l'éponge.	Al circo l'acrobata ogni sera si tuffava da un altezza di venti metri in una spugna bagnata. Poi si ruppe l'osso del collo. Qualcuno aveva strizzato la spugna.	El artista de circo solía saltar desde 15 metros sobre una esponja húmeda. Un día se rompió la cabeza. Alguien había escurrido la esponja.
Carruthers était passionné pour le jeu; chaque fois qu'il avait l'occasion de parier, il ne la ratait pas: aux courses de chevaux, de chiens, au totofoot, aux dés, aux jeux de dominos ou de cartes. Un jour qu'il faisait une partie de cartes avec Forsyth, celui-ci tomba subitement raide mort. Carruthers devait donc annoncer la nouvelle à Mme Forsyth. Il se pointa chez celle-ci et sonna à la porte. Mme Forsyth lui ouvrit. 'Excusez-moi,' lui dit-il, 'mais êtes vous Madame veuve Forsyth?' 'J'suis pas veuve du tout!' 'Comment? Vous faites un pari la-dessus?'	Carruthers aveva la passione del giuoco d'azzardo, e scommetteva sui cavalli, i cani, il totocalcio, i dadi, i domini e le carte. Un giorno mentre stava giuocando a carte con Forsyth, quest'ultimo morí di un colpo. A Carruthers toccò il compito di dare la triste notizia alla signora Forsyth. Suonò alla porta. 'Mi scusi,' disse Carruthers, 'E' lei la vedova Forsyth?' 'Non sono una vedova.' 'E' pronta a farci una scommessa?'	Carruthers era un jugador empedernido que apostaba dinero en cuanto podía: caballos, perros, quinielas, dados, dominó y juegos de naipes. Un día jugaba a las cartas con Forsyth, cuando éste murió de repente. Carruthers fue el encargado de darle la noticia a la señora Forsyth. Esta le abrió en cuanto llamó a la puerta. —Perdone —dijo Carruthers—. ¿Es usted la viuda de Forsyth? —Yo no soy viuda. —¿Le importaría apostar algo, señora?
On demanda à un Chinois ce qu'il pensait des Européens. 'En toute honnêteté,' répondit-il, 'je ne sais pas. Pour moi, ils sont tous pareils.'	Al Cinese fu chiesto che cosa pensasse degli Europei. 'Francamente, non potrei dirlo. A me sembrano tutti uguali.'	A un chino le preguntaron su opinión sobre los europeos. —Honradamente, no lo sé —dijo—. Todos me parecen iguales.

GERMAN

Smith went in to complain to his tailor that he couldn't sit down in his new trousers.
'But you asked for them to be skin-tight,' said the tailor.
'True,' said Smith. 'But I can sit down in my skin—I can't in these trousers.'

Smith beschwert sich bei seinem Schneider, er könne in der neuen Hose nicht sitzen.
'Sie wollten Sie hauteng haben,' verteitigt sich der Schneider, 'und dann wundern Sie sich, wenn Sie nicht drin sitzen können.'
'Wundert mich auch, denn in meiner Haut kann ich sehr gut sitzen.'

The Irish astronaut was telling his friend about Ireland's space programme.
'We're not bothering at all with the moon,' he said. 'We're flying to the sun.'
'The sun!' exclaimed his friend. 'But if you get within fifty thousand miles of it, your spaceship will just melt away.'
'We've thought of that,' said the astronaut. 'We're going at night.'

Der irische Astronaut erklärte einem Freund Irlands Raumforschungsprogramm.
'Wir halten uns erst gar nicht beim Mond auf, fliegen gleich zur Sonne.'
'Zur Sonne?' ruft sein Freund entgeistert. 'Unmöglich! Euer Raumschiff würde bereits schmilzen, wenn Ihr noch fünfzigtausend Meilen entfernt seid!'
'Haben wir alles schon überlegt,' sagt der Ire, 'das machen wir in der Nacht.'

The deep-sea diver was being attacked by man-eating sharks.
'Can I come up? Can I come up?' he signalled to the boat above.
'It's hardly worth it,' came the message back. 'We're sinking.'

Ein Tiefseetaucher wird von einem Haifisch angegriffen.
'Hilfe! Ich komme rauf!' signalisierte er zum Boot.
'Bleib unten, wir sinken!' kam die Antwort zurück.

FRENCH	ITALIAN	SPANISH
Smith alla voir son tailleur et se plaignit qu'il ne pouvait pas s'asseoir dans le nouveau pantalon qu'il s'était fait faire. 'Mais vous le vouliez tellement étroit qu'il devait littéralement vous coller à la peau!' déclara le tailleur. 'D'accord!' répondit Smith; 'mais ma peau ne me gêne pas pour m'asseoir; le pantalon, si!'	Smith si recò dal sarto per lamentarsi che i pantaloni che gli aveva confezionato erano cosí stretti da non permettergli di sedersi. 'Ma se è stata lei a chiedermi di farglieli aderenti come una seconda pelle!' disse il sarto. 'Già, ma la mia pelle mi permette di sedermi!'	Smith fué a quejarse al sastre de que no podía sentarse con los pantalones nuevos. —Pero usted me pidió que le quedaran tirantes como la piel —dijo el sastre. —¡Cierto! —contestó Smith—. Pero con la piel puedo sentarme y con esos pantalones, no.
L'astronaute irlandais exposait à son ami le programme spatial de l'Irlande. 'On va laisser carrément de côté la lune,' dit-il, 'et on va aller droit au soleil.' 'Le soleil!' s'ecria son ami. 'Mais si vous vous approchez à moins de 80 mille kilomètres du soleil, votre vaisseau spatial va fondre comme de la cire!' 'On y a pensé,' répliqua l'astronaute; 'alors, on va y aller de nuit!'	L'astronauta irlandese stava parlando ad un amico del programma spaziale irlandese. 'A noi non ce ne importa proprio niente della luna!' disse. 'Andremo sul sole.' 'Sul sole!' esclamò l'amico. 'Ma non sai che ad una distanza di ottantamila chilometri l'astronave si scioglierà come una candela accesa?' 'Già, ci abbiamo pensato,' rispose l'astronauta, 'e perciò ci andremo di notte.'	Un astronauta irlandés le contaba a su amigo el programa espacial de Irlanda. —No vamos a preocuparnos de la Luna —dijo—. ¡Volaremos hacia el Sol! —¿Hacia el Sol? —exclamó su amigo—. Pero si os acercáis a cincuenta mil millas, vuestra nave espacial se derritirá. —Ya hemos pensado en eso —contestó el astronauta—. ¡Iremos de noche!
Le plongeur sous-marin était menacé par de féroces requins. 'Puis-je remonter à la surface? Vite! Puis-je remonter?' lança-t-il sur sa radio portative. 'Pas la peine,' répondit le capitaine du vaisseau, 'on est en train de couler.'	Un sommozzatore era stato attaccato da un branco di rapaci pescecani. 'Posso tornare a bordo?' segnalò alla barca che lo seguiva. 'Non ne vale la pena,' fu la risposta. 'Stiamo affondando.'	Al buceador de alta mar le atacaban los tiburones. —¿Puedo subir? ¿puedo subir? —transmitió al buque nodriza. —No creo que valga la pena —fue el mensaje que recibió—. ¡Nos estamos hundiendo!

GERMAN

A burly, unshaven cowhand walked into the wild west saloon, where the pianist was playing the honky-tonk piano.
'Hey, Broken Nose,' said the cowboy, 'can't you play some other tune?'
'Whaddya mean, Broken Nose?' said the pianist. 'I haven't got a broken nose.'
A great hairy fist flew through the air and landed with a sickening thud.
'O.K., O.K.,' said the pianist through a bloodstained handkerchief. 'What would you like to hear?'

In der Wildwest-Bar klimpert der Pianist seine Tingeltangel-Musik. Ein kräftiger unrasierte Cowboy betritt die Bar.
'Du, Krummnase, kannst Du nichts besseres spielen?' fährt er den Klavierspieler an.
'Was heisst hier Krummnase! Erlauben Sie 'mal . . . meine Nase ist . . .'
Eine haarige Faust unterbricht seinen Satz.
'Meine Nase war immer ganz gerade,' wimmert der Pianist blutüberströmt, '. . . und was möchten Sie hören?'

'I've got all my clothes off, doctor. Where shall I put them?'
'On top of mine, madam. On top of mine . . .'

'Ich habe alles ausgezogen, Herr Doktor, wo kann ich meine Sachen hinlegen?'
'Auf meine, gnädige Frau.'

The scientist worked for years on a liquid that would dissolve anything. Finally he perfected it. Metal, stone, wood, glass, plastic—anything, in fact, that the liquid touched, immediately dissolved.
Then the scientist committed suicide out of sheer frustration. He couldn't find anything to keep the liquid in.

Seit Jahren experimentierte der Wissenschaftler, um eine Flüssigkeit zu erfinden, mit der alles aufgelöst werden kann. Schliesslich hatte er Erfolg. Metall, Stein, Glas, Holz, alles konnte völlig vernichtet werden, sobald es mit dieser Flüssigkeit in Berührung kam. Dann nahm sich der Wissenschaftler aus Verzweiflung das Leben, denn es gab nichts, worin er die Flüssigkeit aufbewahren konnte.

FRENCH	ITALIAN	SPANISH
Hirsute et trapu, le cow-boy entra dans un bar du Far-West où un pianiste était en train de jouer un ragtime endiablé. 'Hé! Nez de Travers!' dit le cow-boy, 'tu peux pas jouer aut'chose?' 'Kékcé qu'tu veux dire Nez de Travers?' demanda le pianiste. 'J'ai pas le Nez de Travers!' Un énorme poing velu atterrit sur sa face avec un bruit sourd. 'Ça va, ça va,' dit le pianiste à travers un mouchoir tout ensanglanté, 'qu'est ce que vous voulez que je joue?'	Un grosso cow-boy barbuto entrò in un bar del Far West, dove un pianista stava strimpellando una canzonetta. 'Tu, Faccia da Schiaffi,' disse al pianista, non puoi suonare qualche cos'altro?' 'Che cosa vuoi dire, Faccia da Schiaffi?' chiese il pianista. 'Io non ho una faccia da schiaffi.' Una grossa mano pelosa attraversò l'aria e si posò sul viso del pianista con un colpo da far paura. 'Va bene, va bene,' disse il pianista attraverso un fazzoletto intriso di sangue, 'e che cosa vorresti sentire?'	Un vaquero fornido, con el rostro sin afeitar, entró en un 'saloon' del salvaje Oeste, en el que un pianista tocaba un desafinado piano. —¡Eh, nariz rota! —exclamó el vaquero—. ¿No podrías tocar cualquier otra musiquilla? —¿Qué quiere decir, nariz rota? —dijo el pianista—. ¡Yo no tengo la nariz rota! Un enorme y velloso puño cruzó el aire y se estrelló con un escalofriante chasquido. —¡Está bien, está bien! —dijo el pianista a través de un ensangrentado pañuelo—. ¿Qué es lo que le gustaría escuchar?
'Voilà, docteur, j'ai enlevé tous mes vêtements. Où dois-je les mettre?' 'Sur les miens, Madame, sur les miens . . .'	'Dottore, mi sono spogliata comptetamente. Dove devo mettere gli indumenti?' 'Sui miei, signora, sui miei. . .'	—Ya me he desvestido, doctor. ¿Dónde dejo mis ropas? —Encima de las mías, señora. Encima de las mías . . .
Pendant des années, le savant avait travaillé à mettre au point la formule d'un liquide capable de dissoudre n'importe quoi. Enfin, il y arriva. Métal, pierre, bois, verre, plastique . . . bref, tout ce que le liquide touchait était immédiatement dissous. Et c'est alors que le savant se suicida de désespoir, ne trouvant rien qui puisse contenir son liquide.	Per anni uno scienziato studiò per trovare un liquido che dissolvesse qualsiasi cosa. Alla fine lo perfezionò. Metallo, pietra, legno, vetro, plastica, qualsiasi cosa insomma che veniva in contatto con il liquido si dissolveva immediatamente Poi lo scienziato si suicidò per disperazione, non potendo trovare un recipiente in cui conservare il liquido.	El sabio había trabajado durante muchos años para conseguir un líquido que lo disolviera todo. Finalmente lo perfeccionó: el metal, las piedras, la madera, el cristal, el plástico, todo, de hecho, lo que el líquido tocaba, se disolvía inmediatamente. Entonces el sabio se suicidó de pura desesperación. No podía hallar nada donde conservar el líquido.

GERMAN

The man rang up his dim friend at three o'clock in the morning. The 'phone rang and rang and finally a very sleepy voice answered 'Hello?'
'I'm sorry to wake you up at this time,' said the man.
'That's all right,' said his dim friend, 'I had to get up to answer the 'phone anyway.'

Ein Mann ruft seinen Freund nachts um drei Uhr an. Das Telefon läutet eine ganze Weile. Dann antwortet eine verschlafene Stimme:
'Hallo?'
'Es tut mir sehr leid, dass ich Dich um diese Zeit aufwecke,' sagt der Mann.
'Schon gut, ich musste ja sowieso das Telefon antworten.'

A revolutionary was being consoled in his cell by the priest a few minutes before he was due to face the firing squad.
'Have you any last request?' asked the priest.
'Can I ask for anything at all?'
'Anything within reason, my son,' said the priest.
'What about something special to wear in front of the firing squad?'
'No trouble at all. I'll see to it right away. What would you like?'
'If it's not too much trouble, father—a steel helmet and a bullet-proof vest.'

'Haben Sie noch einen Wunsch, mein Sohn?' fragte der Priester den Revolutionär kurz vor der Hinrichtung.
'Kann ich mir wünschen was ich will?'
'Es muss im Rahmen der Möglichkeit sein, mein Sohn.'
'Ich möchte gern etwas besonderes bei meiner Hinrichtung tragen.'
'Der Wunsch kann erfüllt werden; ich kümmere mich sofort darum. Was möchten Sie anziehen?'
'Wenn es nicht zuviel Mühe macht, hätte ich gern einen Stahlhelm und eine kugelfeste Jacke.'

FRENCH

L'homme téléphona à trois heures du matin à son ami qui n'était pas très fort du ciboulot.
Le téléphone sonna longtemps avant qu'enfin une voix toute ensommeilée dise à l'autre bout du fil: 'Allo?'
'Je m'excuse d'avoir à te réveiller à une heure pareille,' dit l'homme à son ami.
'Ça fait rien,' dit le simplet, 'il fallait bien que je me lève de toute façon pour répondre au téléphone.'

ITALIAN

Un uomo telefonò ad un amico alle tre di mattina. Il telefono squillò a lungo e, finalmente, una voce insonnolita rispose 'Pronto'.
'Mi dispiace svegliarti a quest'ora,' disse l'uomo.
'Oh, non stare a preoccuparti,' rispose l'amico, 'tanto dovevo alzarmi lo stesso per rispondere al telefono.'

SPANISH

Un hombre telefoneó a su amigo a las tres de la madrugada.
El aparato sonó y sonó, hasta que al fin una voz soñolienta respondió:
—¡Dígame!
—Perdóname —dijo el primero— que te haya hecho levantar a estas horas.
—¡No importa! —contestó el amigo—. Tenía que levantarme de todas formas para contestar el teléfono.

Dans la cellule du condamné, le prêtre prodigait ses encouragements au révolutionnaire qui allait passer dans quelques minutes devant le peloton d'exécution.
'Avez-vous un dernier souhait à formuler?' demanda le prêtre.
'Puis-je demander n'importe quoi?'
'N'importe quoi pourvu que ça soit raisonnable,' répondit le prêtre.
'Même si je veux m'habiller spécialement avant de passer devant le peloton d'exécution?'
'Pas de problème pour la question vestimentaire. Je m'en occuperai moi-même immédiatement. Que voulez-nous mettre?'
'Si c'est pas trop d'ennui, mon père, je voudrais un casque en acier et un gilet anti-balles; s'il vous plaît.'

Un prete stava consolando un rivoluzionario pochi minuti prima che questo venisse accompagnato davanti al plotone di esecuzione.
'Ha un ultimo desiderio?' domandò il prete.
'Posso chiedere qualsiasi cosa?'
'Nei limiti del possibile, figlio mio,' disse il prete.
'Anche qualche cosa di speciale da indossare davanti al plotone di esecuzione?'
'Certamente. Me ne occuperò subito. Che cosa vorrebbe?'
'Se non è di troppo disturbo, padre, un elmetto di acciaio e una corazza.'

Un revolucionario era confortado en su celda por el capellán, pocos minutos antes de ser conducido ante el piquete de ejecución.
—¿Tienes algún último deseo? —le preguntó el capellán.
—¿Puedo pedir cualquier cosa?
—Siempre que sea algo razonable, hijo mío —repuso el cura.
—¿Qué le parece, algo especial para vestirme frente al piquete de ejecución?
—No hay inconveniente. Procuraré complacerte. ¿Qué quieres llevar?
—Si no es mucha molestia, padre, un casco de acero y un traje a prueba de balas.